MODERN WISDOM, ANCIENT ROOTS

MODERN WISDOM, ANCIENT ROOTS

The Movers and Shakers'
Guide to Unstoppable Success

SRIKUMAR S. RAO

RUPA

Published by
Rupa Publications India Pvt. Ltd 2023
7/16, Ansari Road, Daryaganj
New Delhi 110002

Sales Centres:
Bengaluru Chennai
Hyderabad Jaipur Kathmandu
Kolkata Mumbai Prayagraj

P-ISBN: 978-93-5702-575-1
E-ISBN: 978-93-5702-576-8

First impression 2023

10 9 8 7 6 5 4 3 2 1

Printed in India

To my grandchildren, Krish, Kyra and Nyra

Many centuries ago, Shantideva, Indian philosopher and Buddhist monk, received a penetrating insight into the human predicament. He lamented, 'I do not desire suffering. But, fool that I am, I desire the causes of suffering.' I hope that, someday, this book will help them skirt this pitfall.

If you cry because the sun has gone out of your life,
your tears will prevent you from seeing the stars.

—Rabindranath Tagore

CONTENTS

FOREWORD

On rare occasions, a teacher comes into your life who shakes up your worldview and upends everything you thought you knew. And from this chaos, you emerge stronger, more polished and more confident in handling any curveball that life throws at you.

For me, that teacher is Srikumar Rao.

I have known Srikumar for 11 years, and he has become a mentor, a friend and a man who has helped me see the world in radically different and beautiful new ways. He has given me sage advice that has helped me greatly in my role as CEO of one of the largest companies in the world exclusively dedicated to raising the consciousness of a global population.

Srikumar is an elite coach, working with super achievers. He is one of a tiny number of coaches who can intuitively sense where you are and give you what you truly need. This may not be what you want, but it is what truly benefits you—at that moment and in your life going forward.

Let me give you a personal example.

From 2013 to 2016, my company, Mindvalley, was burning through cash. A series of disastrous events nearly wiped out the business. This three-year period was a battle for survival. One evening, after another horrid day in survival mode, I flopped in distress onto a chair at my kitchen table. I was in crisis. It was 11.00 p.m. I wanted to smash my head into my pillow, turn the lights off and go to sleep.

But I had a call booked with Srikumar to discuss his appearance on one of our popular content shows. Thankfully, I kept the appointment. That night, I experienced his sage wisdom for the first time.

Srikumar is a well-known business professor whose courses have been among the most popular at some of the top business schools in the world. His methods are revolutionary. He mixes the teachings of long-dead philosophers and spiritual teachers with modern, American business school ideas. It's not your classic MBA curriculum. It's more like the love child of Rumi and Jack Welch.

Srikumar lives in New York, but he is not the classically brash New York type. He is a humble, down-to-earth Indian man. He's the kind of person who only occasionally opens his mouth in a group, and he speaks slowly. But whenever he speaks, every person in the room shuts up because they know he's going to blow their mind.

That night he asked me if I was okay. I said I was fine. I may even have said that I was feeling terrific. I don't remember. He knew it was a lie. He's good at reading people.

He probed gently. He struck me as so loving, so sincere, that I felt safe with him. I'd been struggling to hold in my anguish, and now I let it all out in a messy stream of confessions.

'I'm burning out, Dr Rao,' I told him. 'I am stressed out. My health has gone to shit. I am questioning my ability to lead and be a CEO. I am fighting to keep this company above water. And I can't share this with anyone. I've been keeping it all in. And I just don't know what to do.'

He listened patiently. And then he read a poem to me. It

was from the mystic Rumi:

> When I run after what I think I want, my days are a furnace of distress and anxiety; If I sit in my own place of patience, what I need flows to me, and without pain. From this I understand that what I want also wants me, is looking for me and attracting me. There is a great secret here for anyone who can grasp it.*

We talked about the verse and its implications for me and the life I was living. I felt much calmer right away, and began my transition from frantic doing to calm being. It took me years to truly understand the profundity buried in those simple lines.

Srikumar was right. It was exactly what I needed. I just didn't know I needed it.

Subsequently, Srikumar appeared in many Mindvalley programmes. His 'Quest for Personal Mastery' is the highest-rated programme in its series. His talks have overflow audiences. And countless Mindvalley members have tales about how something they learned from him transformed their life.

And he continues to transform my life.

Srikumar once spoke to me of the idea that we should adopt a mental model that we live in a benevolent universe. That we should trust that the world has our back, and that everything that happens to us is for our own good.

I pushed back and asked, 'If this was true, why did I feel that the world was against me, and why was I going through so much failure and pain at work?'

He replied, 'The common misconception, Vishen, is that people think their work is about their work. This is wrong.'

---

*Rumi, *Rumi Poetry: 100 Bedtime Verses* (CreateSpace, 2017), p. 2.

The next piece of wisdom out of his mouth spun me around.

'The most important lesson our business schools need to teach us is that our work is not about our work. Rather, our work is nothing more than the ultimate vehicle for our personal growth. If your business fails, it doesn't matter. The question is, how did you *grow*? If your business becomes a billion-dollar company, it doesn't matter. The question is, how did you *grow*?'

That interaction was a pivotal moment. I started to see new actions I could take to free myself of the torment I was suffering. I certainly was not viewing my predicament from the perspective that it was growing *me* in a new way as a CEO and business owner. This simple context shift gave me instant relief. I began seeing situations that had been keeping me up at night through a new lens of appreciation.

The entire model most societies have for success and happiness is flawed. Most people believe that to attain fulfilment in life, you must acquire three things:

- A certain role or title (which gives you prestige)
- A certain balance in your bank account (which gives you wealth)
- Specific material possessions, such as a car or a house with a white picket fence

The result: success.

Right? Nope! Srikumar would call that the 'if-then life'—one in which you are constantly thinking, *If I get X, then I will be happy*. He says you have to stop hanging your happiness on your title, your money and your stuff. Stop thinking, *I need X to be successful or happy*. (How many times have you got X and *still* not felt happy?) The Rao formula to reclaim your happiness is simply, growth!

The only point of life is to grow. Pain can lead to growth. Success can lead to growth. Look at it this way, and pain ceases to exist. Success ceases to be intoxicating. Growth is the only thing that matters.

Real success is much simpler than most of us have been led to believe. There is nothing you have to *get to* or *be* in order to have finally made it. You just need to keep growing.

It is a pleasure and honour to write this foreword for Srikumar's new book. This book is the next best thing to having him as your personal coach. The chapters are short, but the lessons are profound and life-changing. Implement these lessons, and you will indeed be propelled to unstoppable success.

I wish you great joy as you progress through life.

—Vishen Lakhiani
CEO of Mindvalley

PREFACE

We are sick! I mean *really, really* sick!

We get all agitated about airplane crashes, even though the probability that we will perish in one is vanishingly small. But we ignore the real sickness that is already upon us, that saps our energy every day, that debilitates us and keeps us functioning at a level far below our best and makes us miserable. It drives us to drink, do drugs and to wild pursuits. It even tips many of us off the ledge to commit suicide.

So bad is this sickness that we have a unique way of coping with it.

We simply label it *normal*!

I am being dead serious. To help you understand what I mean, I will ask you a question. Think about it earnestly.

In the past 24 hours, how much time have you spent thinking about your left little finger?

Got the answer? Good. In the past 24 hours you have not thought about your left little finger at all. Perhaps you polished the nail or clipped it. If so, your attention was on it for a few seconds and then you moved on.

Your left little finger was doing what left little fingers do, and you paid it no heed. And that is as it should be. If any part of your body is functioning normally, it does its thing quietly and does not draw attention to itself.

Now, suppose somebody accidentally slammed the car door on your left little finger. You will spend a great deal of time on that little finger in the next 24 hours. In fact, it may dominate your thoughts. It will reach out and demand your attention because it is unwell.

Deeply unwell.

Now, think about your mind. If it was well, it would function silently in the background and do what you set it to do. But look at how it ceaselessly bothers you and draws attention to itself.

Am I too fat?

Why do I find it so difficult to wake up and work out every morning?

What does she really think of me?

Don't want to go to work today—wish I could just lay in bed.

Why doesn't he call me? I thought we had a great date, but it's already been a week and no phone call or email. I guess I'm not that attractive anymore.

Lisa got promoted? She is so dumb. How the hell did that happen? I bet she slept her way to it. That's just the kind of person she is. Nothing I can do about that.

My mom says I never call. Every time I do, she goes on about all the things that are wrong in her life and, before we are done, I wish I could crawl into a hole.

Other people are happily married. Why aren't I? Is there something wrong with me?

Get the picture? That cacophony in your head is your mind drawing attention to itself with its wild imaginings and off-the-wall conjectures. It will not let you be. It forces you to pay heed, and you are so fatigued by it that, in despair, you do anything you can to quiet it.

You turn on the TV. Not because there is something you want to watch, but because you want to distract that horribly sick mind. It cannot rest quietly by itself.

You drink. You do controlled substances. You work ungodly hours. You flit from relationship to relationship to find that 'perfect' one. You check your email every few minutes. You have developed many strategies to cope, and none of them are satisfactory or work consistently.

That is because the sickness is deep.

Do you recognize how troubled you are? Be grateful to your left little finger. It has just taught you a powerful lesson.

The biggest consolation you have is that everybody is equally sick, and some even more so. We label it 'normal'. But it is not so.

You can get rid of this sickness. It will not be easy. It will not be fast. In fact, it will take the rest of your life. Tapping into your inner wisdom to gain fortitude and peace is indeed a lifelong pursuit. There have been stories told about this journey through the ages, and in this book I share some of them with you, beginning with this one.

> There once lived an emperor whose royal duties left him little occasion for contemplation of the deeper mysteries of life. He simply didn't have the time or space to answer questions about why he existed at all and what his purpose was.
>
> So, he charged his vizier to give him short—very short—nuggets that he could ponder. He hoped that this would stir some inspiration within him, and thereby help him become clear about the meaning of existence. His time was limited but his desire was keen.

And that is what this book is designed to do. Each chapter is brief, but the concepts are intended to function like dynamite for your soul. They build on each other to blast your models of the world and take you down the rabbit hole, and out again into a realm of incredible possibility and transcendent joy.

I wish you well on this journey.

1

ENGINEERING CHANGE OVERNIGHT

We are all stuck in our ways.

I wager that on New Year's Eve or on your birthday, you have decided to quit smoking, start exercising regularly, eat healthy and generally straighten out your life.

And, of course, you have failed. We all have.

Many claim that, by the time we reach adulthood, we have been fundamentally shaped and will not change much for the rest of our lives. This notion has been enshrined in our language and in popular culture.

We all know that 'you can't teach an old dog new tricks'. Change rarely happens, right? And if it does, it requires Herculean effort and is slow. Once you become an adult, you are, to a large extent, frozen.

I profoundly disagree with this for a variety of reasons.

You *can* change!

This change can happen dramatically and overnight. And it can be lasting.

Sri Ramakrishna, the nineteenth-century Indian sage, is believed to have asked, 'Imagine a cave sealed in a mountain for thousands of years. Then you remove the rocks that have blocked its entrance. Does the darkness dissipate little by little?

Or does it vanish instantly?'

No matter how many centuries blackness has lingered, it disappears when exposed to light.

No matter how many decades your behaviour has persisted, it can change in an instant. The trick is to learn how to engineer this change.

You cannot do it by force of will.

The way you *can* do it is by changing the mental models you use to view the world. These models cumulatively determine who you are. As you make changes in them, you literally become a different person. Then, everything changes.

A mental model is a notion we have about the way the world works. We have dozens of models, perhaps hundreds of them. We have a model for how to get a job, another for how to get ahead in the job we get, another for how to find a partner and so on. The problem is not that we have mental models. The problem is that we do not recognize that we have mental models. We think the model is reality, and not just a model.

For example, we may believe that the only way to succeed is to get good grades from a good school and then get a good job, work hard and climb the ladder of success. But then we run across figures like Bill Gates and Steve Jobs. We become open to entrepreneurial avenues that would not even have occurred to us before. Let's consider the story of an investment banker whose marriage was going downhill.

> He put in long hours, burning the candle at both ends. Multiple deals were coming to a head simultaneously, and he was barely able to keep his nose above water. When he came home dead tired, his wife would assail him for being late again and 'not caring' about her.

He would snap back that if he did not care about her, he would not put in the hours he did to make the income he earned, which gave them the lifestyle they enjoyed. And then they would fight. He thought she was selfish and self-absorbed.

He confided his woes to the teacher in his meditation class.

'Do you remember the third time you came to mentor the child assigned to you?' the teacher asked.

He did. He was late, and the child ran to him screaming and pounded him on the chest with his small fists. He recognized that the youngster had been looking forward to meeting him all day and was frustrated at the delay. He apologized and held the boy tightly. Then he mimicked the boy and pretended to hit himself while crying out loudly. The child burst out laughing. The banker had done a darn good job of soothing him.

'Can you not see that when your wife attacks you, she is really saying, "I love you. I want to be with you. Why are you not there?" You could understand the frustration of the child. Why can't you see the same thing in your wife?'

That did the trick. When he came home late again and his wife began her tirade, he was able to see it as an expression of loneliness and her desire to be with him. He responded with compassion and gentleness. And she quickly ran out of steam and calmed down. And slowly their marriage started to heal.

That's the way it works. When you change your mental model of how the world works, the changes happen right away. You change. The world changes.

A small tweak in a mental model can make a huge difference in your experience of life.

It is not always easy to recognize the mental models you hold, so there is hard work required to identify them. But once you have done so, you can make changes in them. And you'll find that a small tweak in a mental model can make a huge difference in your experience of life.

2

A LIFE LESSON FROM MUNDANE CHORES

We were in Paris one summer and my wife, who is a big Monet fan, dragged me to Monet's home in Giverny. Monet was one of those rare painters who actually made enough money during his lifetime to live a comfortable, even luxurious, life.

Monet's garden is unbelievably lush with flowers of every imaginable colour. Some beds have identical blossoms, as neatly arrayed as soldiers in uniform. Others have a plethora of blooms of different varieties and hues, and their studied contrast makes them pleasing to the eye. There are climbing roses, long-stemmed hollyhocks, coloured banks of annuals and curving walkways that take you over bridges and under trellises festooned with vines and climbing flowers. There are rhododendrons and tulips and crocuses and daisies and dahlias. There are benches scattered all over the estate, and you can sit on any one of them and think peaceful thoughts. The atmosphere is highly conducive to doing so.

My wife was inspired and tried to recreate this beauty in our backyard. She succeeded in large measure. And, indeed, I do sit in my backyard and think peaceful thoughts and contemplate the meaning of life.

I was under the impression that a beautiful garden like this just happens. You kind of wish it into being. Last week, my wife asked me to help her spread mulch around the flowerbeds. And she asked me to help her weed before that.

I found out that gardens *don't just happen.* I was sweating profusely within 20 minutes and fled indoors precipitously after another half hour because I had important phone calls to make.

Think about this.

Your mind is the most fertile garden that you will ever see. It *will* bring forth.

Your mind is the most fertile garden that you will ever see. It will bring forth.

Whether it becomes a picturesque Eden or an overgrown mess depends on how conscientiously you do the weeding. The unfortunate part is that because the soil is so incredibly fertile, the weeds grow fast and in profusion along with the crops and flowers you want.

Watch your mind as you go through the day:

You catch sight of *Forbes*—the 400 issue—on the newsstand and think, *Why can't I be as rich as that?*

You spy a really good-looking woman and wonder, *Is she married?* And momentarily forget that you are.

Your boss criticizes your last report, and you mentally consign her to Gitmo or, even better, a rendition camp in Poland.

Weeds, weeds, weeds.

Thousands of them spring up every day, and you are not even aware of when or why they appear. And, because of this, they take root and grow big.

This is where and how your many addictions and destructive thought patterns originate. They bedevil you, besiege you, beset you and rob you of peace and equanimity.

If you are ruthlessly diligent about the weeding, you absolutely will create a splendid garden. The human condition is messy, just like the untamed rambling brush and scrub that needs clearing. But there is a way to straighten out your life.

A similar lesson can also up from doing your laundry. I ran low on underwear a few days ago. And I ran out of the comfortable sweats and hoodies that I like to live in, when at home. So, I did my laundry.

I don't like doing laundry. Once upon a time, I really hated it. Now I don't, but it is not one of my favourite ways of spending time. If I were to make a list of five activities that really energize me, doing laundry would not be one of them. I do it because I have to and because I need fresh clothes.

It felt good when I saw the empty hamper and realized that all my clothes were washed, folded and put away, ready for use. But the hamper did not remain empty. There were dirty clothes in it the next morning, and I just added today's quota.

Soon I will have to do my laundry again.

Weeds come up in our fertile garden and when we pluck them out, they reappear. Our hamper is empty when we do our laundry, but then the dirty clothes start piling up.

Our inner life is just like that.

Our errant mental chatter constitutes the weeds that choke it. This mental chatter has innumerable sources. We are angry at others and ourselves. We covet wealth and fame and power. We are jealous and lustful. We are driven by ambition and riven by pain.

The human condition is messy.

We meditate and achieve clarity. We clearly see that we are pursuing ends that will complicate our lives and bring us sorrow in the end. We root out those weeds.

But the weeds will come back.

The laundry hamper will fill up again.

Clothes don't stay clean forever once you wash them. They will get dirty again. And again. So, you wash them again. And again.

The clarity that you achieve after a good meditation will leave you, and you will revert to being an ego-driven automaton, jerked about by fickle desires. Doing the laundry is not a one-time action. Achieving clarity of purpose and serenity in life is not a one-and-done proposition.

So, keep meditating, keep reflecting and, above all, continue to seek out aids to keep your conscious mind on your spiritual quest. These aids might include like-minded friends, books, audio and video material, retreats, smartphone apps and much else.

Make all this a permanent part of your life.

Like laundry.

3

THE MARVELLOUS PRISON BOXING YOU IN

How do you view the many positive and negative events that befall you? Howsoever you paint the picture, that view ultimately determines how you experience life itself. And yes, you are in prison—you just don't know it. Let's take the following story as an example.

> There lived a man who was a respected sage, a teacher of many generations of students. No one could match him in knowledge of philosophy and the sacred texts. He lived simply with his family in the remote countryside.
>
> One of his students, who had achieved great fame and fortune in the court of the king, came to visit him. As the student paid his respects, he noted the threadbare clothes of his teacher and the sparse larder.
>
> 'Revered Sir,' he said, overcome with emotion, 'please come with me to the capital. The king will shower you with wealth because there is no one to match you in wisdom. All you have to do is praise His Majesty and you will no longer have to subsist on lentils.'

Tears rolled down the old preceptor's face. 'My son,' said the sage, 'is this all you have learned in the years you spent with me? Do you not see that if you would learn to subsist on lentils, you would not have to praise His Majesty?'

Krista Tippett, creator of the *On Being* podcast, told me of her early days with the American Embassy in divided Germany. I was particularly struck by an insight she shared from those final days of the Cold War in Berlin. She had good friends on both sides of the Wall and noted that West Berliners were heavily subsidized and had access to all manner of material goods. In the West, there was consumer plenty. In the East, there was drab sameness; people could not paint their houses with the colour of their choice, or even choose their college major.*

But the East Berliners improvised. Poetry could not be published, so they created poetry circles that fostered community and nourished the spirit. Friends and family were more important in East Berlin, and people invested in them. The 'free' Germans, on the other hand, had impoverished inner lives. Krista's friends on the Soviet Bloc side led lives of dignity and purpose, while the West Berliners were anxiety-ridden in their material plenty.

Observations like this were partly responsible for Krista starting her enormously successful podcast. And that reminded me of a comment made by one of the participants in my programme who had come of age in communist Hungary. We would consider the lives he and his friends led 'bleak'.

---

*Rao, Srikumar, 'If You Build It, Will They Come?', *Inc.*, 28 February 2017, https://tinyurl.com/2xhmrmsf. Accessed on 8 August 2023.

'We all wore the same clothes, all the houses looked the same and our entertainment choices were limited,' he noted. But, on reflection, he added, 'I have to say that most people I know were happier then than they are now.'

I am emphatically not saying that we should go back to communist rule, with entire populations subject to the whims of autocrats.

I am saying that we have notions about 'freedom' and 'happiness' that are flat-out wrong. I am saying that in pursuing external freedoms so fiercely, we have actually lost a much greater freedom. I am making a case for you to look at your life.

As a country and society, we are obsessed with freedom. We view it as an inalienable right. We are ready to fight—and die—for it. We think we have it and have to protect it because it is fragile and can be stripped from us. In our minds, freedom is essential for happiness.

Perhaps.

But our thinking about what freedom is and how to get it may be in error. It may be dead wrong. And this could be costing us dearly in terms of happiness.

We have codified laws that guarantee us freedom of speech and worship and assembly. We wrangle endlessly about other freedoms, such as the right to bear arms or choose the gender of our partners or terminate a pregnancy.

But we define 'freedom' too narrowly.

We equate freedom with the elimination of restrictions on our behaviour. In our relentless pursuit of this goal, we are reordering society, smashing traditions and taboos alike. Sexual preoccupation is reaching new highs, along with acceptance of its flaunting. Illegal drugs are more powerful and chemically complex. Our popular entertainment constantly stretches and snaps boundaries of taste and propriety. We have become marvellously adept at titillating our jaded senses.

However, there is another type of 'freedom' that we have not achieved and are barely pursuing.

We are still prey to the ruthless harpies of desire that constantly spur us into action, ignite avarice and overweening ambition and goad us into activities that consume all our available time and more. We are driven by our demons, all of us—takeover titan and veteran employee; corporate chieftain and newly-minted MBA; serial killer and confidence trickster; presidential candidate and congressional intern.

We are all in the fierce grip of our restless minds, being blown hither and thither like a tumbleweed in a tornado.

The talons of our addictions shred our minds and wreck repose.

Some, like cocaine, we declare illegal and expend vast resources to counteract. Others, like workaholism, we applaud and reward. Still others, like hypochondria and gambling, we barely acknowledge.

Like it or not, we are all in the fierce grip of our restless minds, being blown hither and thither like a tumbleweed in a tornado, expending our psychic energies in emotional rollercoasters that we are helpless to stop and unable to leave. This, too, is a prison and in our saner moments we want out. As Oscar Wilde describes in 'The Ballad of Reading Gaol':

> I never saw a man who looked
> With such a wistful eye
> Upon that little tent of blue
> Which prisoners call the sky,
> And at every wandering cloud that trailed
> Its raveled fleeces by.

We give to others the power to determine our happiness and tranquility and do not even recognize that we have done so. How 'free' are we really if we cannot sit quietly by ourselves for half an hour?

How free are you really if you cannot quiet your mind without the opiate of your TV or small screen?

It need not be so. There is an alternative to the maelstroms in our mind that we both cultivate and fear. This alternative permits us to be far more efficient and composed. It greatly increases the probability of 'success' in any endeavour and cushions us mightily against the slings and arrows of outrageous fortune.

But, there is a catch. We have to be willing to live in a different mental world and adopt a different outlook on life. In *A Separate Reality*, Don Juan—Carlos Castaneda's mysterious Yaqui warrior—summarizes the viewpoint of a 'man of knowledge':

> A man of knowledge chooses a path with heart and follows it; and then he looks and rejoices and laughs; and then he *sees* and knows. He knows that his life will be over altogether too soon; he knows that he, as well as everybody else, is not going anywhere; he knows, because he *sees*, that nothing is more important than anything else. In other words, a man of knowledge has no honor, no dignity, no family, no name, no country, but only life to be lived, and under these circumstances his only tie to his fellow men is his controlled folly. Thus a man of knowledge endeavors, and sweats, and puffs, and if one looks at him he is just like any ordinary man, except that the folly of his life is under control. Nothing being more important than anything else, a man of knowledge

> chooses any act, and acts it out as if it matters to him. His controlled folly makes him say that what he does matters and makes him act as if it did, and yet he knows that it doesn't; so when he fulfills his acts he retreats in peace, and whether his acts were good or bad, or worked or didn't, is in no way part of his concern.*

It is indeed possible to live a life of great accomplishment and inner harmony. So, if you want to find true freedom, start cutting the tethers—and many of them are electronic—that bind you. And then, like the poet Richard Lovelace wrote in 'To Althea, from Prison' you may discover:

> Stone walls do not a prison make,
> Nor iron bars a cage:
> Minds innocent and quiet take
> That for an hermitage.
> If I have freedom in my love,
> And in my soul am free,
> Angels alone, that soar above,
> Enjoy such liberty.
> And this is precisely the liberty that can be yours,
> if you so choose.

*Casteneda, Carlos, *A Separate Reality: Further Conversations with Don Juan*, Simon and Schuster, 1971.

4

THE DEMON THAT WILL NOT LET YOU BE

On his fifth voyage, Sinbad the Sailor encountered the Old Man of the Sea. Sinbad generously hoisted the Old Man on his shoulders to take him to his destination. But then the Old Man would not let Sinbad go. He locked his legs around Sinbad's neck and forced the unfortunate sailor to take him wherever he wanted. He beat Sinbad with a stave and did not let him rest for a minute.

You, too, have an Old Man who will not let you be. Most of us do. You can probably identify the Old Man in the individuals that surround you in your daily life, even those you are closest to.

Take Sarah, for instance, who had just broken up with her boyfriend when she attended my Creativity and Personal Mastery programme. It had been six months, but the wound was still raw. She could not sleep. She could not focus.

Memories haunted her. We had ice cream for dessert and she burst out crying, remembering an enchanted weekend in Aruba where it had been so hot that she and her boyfriend had literally climbed into a tub of discarded ice cream and had messy fun.

Everything reminded her of him. She dreaded evenings

because they used to cuddle and watch movies. She shunned cheesecake because he used to splurge on it. She stopped going to the gym because he was a fitness nut and worked out regularly. She lost weight. Her boss warned her that her work was unsatisfactory and told her she had to improve.

Her mental chatter was her Old Man of the Sea. So is yours.

Seriously, can you even remember the last time when nothing was bothering you? There is always something. Your career, your health, your in-laws, your children, the environment, your congressman, your partner, your boss, your colleagues.

Seriously, can you even remember the last time when nothing was bothering you?

The world is what it is. It pays no attention to your fervent wishes regarding how it *should* be. And you bend yourself into a pretzel trying to shape it to the way you would like it to be. In the meantime, you carry around a ball and chain.

There is a way out. You can drop your burden.

It is simple, but it is not easy. It is so important, that it is the first exercise I assign to my coaching clients and participants in the programmes I run.

Watch your mental chatter. Observe it. Sarah eventually got to the point where she could detach and watch herself pine for her companion.

When she became a witness of her mental chatter rather than someone mixed up with and carried away by it, the pain eased. And then it went away.

That is how you, too, can free yourself of the denizen perched on your shoulder and refusing to let you go.

5

THE KEY TO GLORIOUS FREEDOM

A character in a movie I saw a long time ago lived in very constricted quarters. He had a narrow cupboard and had to pile all his possessions in it. He balanced his belongings one on top of another in a precarious stack and eventually was afraid to open the door because everything would come tumbling out.

Our lives are like that. We have our likes and dislikes, our fervent desires, our worries for the future, our guilt over many sins of omission and commission, along with a hodgepodge of emotions, memories and experiences. We mash all of these in some manner to create the life we experience. It is a fragile structure, and a sharp knock can bring it all tumbling down.

I thought of that movie when I met Sally.

Sally was unhappy at work. On good days she disliked what she did, and was just able to tolerate her colleagues. On bad days, she loathed her company, detested her coworkers and dreamed of making a doll with the likeness of her boss's face and sticking pins in it. She half-seriously considered taking a voodoo course online to perfect her skill in this.

She was very well-compensated and a single mom. She was unsure of her ability to make the same kind of money elsewhere, so she was circumspect in her behaviour and her language. She did not rock the boat and she placated everybody. In meetings, she found herself agreeing to action items she felt were inadvisable and laughing at jokes she found inappropriate. She smiled when she did not feel like it and mouthed platitudes. She was a good worker and was in no danger of being fired. But she died a little bit every day.

She felt stuck.

Can you relate to Sally's situation in any part of your life? It does not have to be work-related. It could be your marriage. Or relationships with your children, in-laws or relatives. Or what you expected your life would be like. Or all of these.

Fear is a thing. It is a tangible entity that frightens us.

Sally did not consciously think about the entire chain of what could happen, but she was deathly afraid of losing her job and therefore, her health insurance; of being bankrupt because her daughter fell ill and thereby, being forced to leave her comfortable Manhattan apartment and move in with her parents; and...

This is not the world she expected or wanted to live in.

But, let's pause for a moment and look at her life.

Who decided that a spacious Manhattan apartment was desirable and needed for happiness? Who decided that getting a certain salary and living a particular lifestyle was the way to go?

Sally did!

In all likelihood, she did not even realize that she had made all those decisions about what was needed in her life to make it satisfactory. If she really started to dig into the nest of assumptions on which she rested her persona, her life may have crumbled.

It is exactly like opening the crowded cupboard and having all the items you stuffed inside come spilling out.

So, Sally does not open the door and instead huddles fearfully in the restricted space she has created. She does not want to be disturbed by the wholesale change that could happen if she opens the door even a crack.

We all cower, frightened in that small room we have constructed with our fears and imaginings.

I do the same thing. So do you. So does everyone else. We all cower, frightened in that small room we have constructed with our fears and imaginings.

I am not advocating that you open that door. Not yet.

But I am advocating that you recognize that you have a closet you have stuffed full of your life experience and beliefs and that you are afraid to open.

And that is why you are so full of fear.

Think about it. Then think about it again. And again.

Take out your worst fear and examine it ruthlessly, in bright sunshine, and make peace with it.

And enjoy the sense of freedom and exhilaration this brings you.

And Sally? She reached a point where she could not take it anymore. Mentally, she accepted that she could be fired and was prepared to move to rural Wisconsin and work as a teacher. She spoke up at the next all-hands meeting and protested that the project the company was about to fund was ill-conceived.

She was not fired. In fact, she was promoted.

6

WHAT A FOOL HE WAS. OR WAS HE?

It was a sad occasion, but also a festive one. Ted had passed away swiftly and with little suffering. A slight pain in the chest, some difficulty breathing. His wife called 911, and the ambulance rushed him to the hospital but he was gone before it reached the emergency bay.

He looked peaceful in the coffin. Throngs of visitors who had come to pay their final respects, and to say goodbye, were chatting animatedly about how he had helped them in so many ways over so many years.

His mother-in-law stood next to me, so I offered my condolences. I ventured the hope that he was doing well in a better life.

'I hope so,' she replied sharply. 'He certainly wasted this one.' It struck a jarring note, so I probed a bit.

She was forthcoming. 'He was a dreamer,' she said bitterly. 'Always trying to make a big score. Failed at everything he tried and laughed it off. Why didn't he stick to his well-paying job instead of chasing dreams? My daughter and her children paid the price.'

She held forth at length, harping on his many faults and

his inability to match the corporate income he had walked away from.

A half hour later, I spied Ted's wife alone and again offered my sympathies. I couldn't help mentioning my earlier conversation. I wanted to know how she felt.

'Oh, that's my mother!' she said easily. 'She will never understand. I am so thankful that he quit that horrid job. It was sucking his soul dry. After he left, he made less money but was so much more cheerful and fun to be with. We had a wonderful decade.'

She smiled wistfully as she walked back through memory lane. He had been a managing director and a senior partner at a well-known consulting firm. His name was often in the local papers, and he was a substantial citizen in his community.

Ted was not much in demand when he quit to form his own consultancy. Clients did not come in droves. Reporters stopped seeking him out for his views on current happenings. He was no longer invited to big local events, and he did not receive complimentary tickets to performances.

His mother-in-law saw him as a 'failure' for making a 'foolish mistake'.

His wife saw it differently. She saw more of him after he resigned from his high-pressure position, and his temperament was better. He was able to spend more time with his children, in the few years they had, before they went away to college.

He did not have many clients because he was selective, but he genuinely enjoyed working with those he accepted. They were profuse in their appreciation for his efforts. Ted and his wife could not afford expensive vacations anymore, but they were never close to starving.

'If I could go back and do it all over again, I'd have made him quit earlier,' she said.

Too many of us are stuck in some variation of this dilemma. We toil in occupations we find distasteful and judge our success based on the toys we accumulate, rather than on the well-being we experience.

Paul Graham, in his wonderful essay on how to do what you love, warns about the dangers of prestige.* Prestige is a distorting force that makes you want to like something that you really do not. I know many who are caught in this coil.

Prestige is a distorting force that makes you want to like something that you really do not.

One way out is to do what my friend did and walk away.

Another is to genuinely like, not 'pretend like', where you are and what you do.

Look at your own life. How do you define success? Do you do it by markers that others celebrate, such as position, power, money and the like? Or do you do it by internal markers, such as a deep feeling of well-being, joy and sense of purpose?

*'How to Do What You Love,' *Paul Graham*, January 2006, https://tinyurl.com/486sh8rs. Accessed on 8 August 2023.

7

THE GREAT SECRET

One of the blessings of what I do is that people share their deepest longings and darkest fears with me. I am the repository of many confidences, and know the turmoil that lurks beneath many shiny 'success' stories.

One problem, in particular, bedevils many.

They toil in jobs that they mildly dislike or feel disenchanted about and sometimes even hate. They would like to follow their 'passion' but feel stuck because 'they need the income' and can't see how their 'passion' can provide this.

Earlier, I spoke about Ted who found a solution to this dilemma by walking away. I also said that another solution is to really like—not 'pretend like'—what you actually do.

The question is: How do you 'like' or even 'love' something you have spent so much time decrying as something you are stuck in, something you have to 'endure' because of some external consideration such as money, stability or security?

The way to do this is to change the way you think!

You can, in fact, make a quantum leap in life without working harder.

Here is a truth that you may not wish to hear—but think about it all the same. Passion does not exist in the job. It exists in *you.* And if you cannot ignite it within yourself right where you are now, you will not find it outside yourself.

Passion does not exist in the job. It exists in you.

We find what we do distasteful for a number of reasons—the task is boring, meaningless, too tough or too easy. Or we don't like the people with whom we work. Or we resent the time demands. Or we feel that too much is being put on our plate. And speaking of plates, you have had it with the bland cafeteria food but your job has you too mentally fatigued to bring your own lunch.

Each of these is a thought in our head.

It is important to recognize this. Clouds in the sky will be blown away and replaced with other clouds. Our thoughts will similarly dissipate to be replaced with others. They have no power to drag us into dark emotional domains, unless we give them that power.

Try this experiment. The next time you find yourself resenting something at your place of work, see how much of your resistance is caused by your mental chatter telling you, 'I don't want to do this. Why do I have to do this? It's a waste of time. It's beneath me. I should be doing something else…'

See how strong your preferences are and how they drag you willy-nilly into dark places.

Can you start to see your situation as a training ground to disentangle yourself from your ever-so-strong desires? Could this outlook possibly lead to results that are far better than you could have ever imagined?

Many decades ago, a friend who was president of the largest entertainment conglomerate in the world, reminisced about his career.

When he graduated from Harvard Business School, he joined a brokerage firm. It was not his first choice, but it was the only job he could get. He was an analyst, but he didn't get to cover the then-prestigious industries such as automobiles, pharmaceuticals or steel. Instead, he was given the entertainment industry.

In those days, entertainment wasn't even considered an industry, and he was pretty much the only one covering it. This was not what he wanted but he accepted it, more grudgingly than cheerfully.

Gradually, he made his peace with his new position.

He set himself to become knowledgeable about motion pictures, recorded music, leisure and recreational trends. He liked the people he met and became interested in what they were doing and why they were doing it.

Soon, strong-willed entrepreneurs like Steve Ross, Lew Wasserman and Charles Bluhdorn built up holding companies into conglomerates such as Warner Communications, Music Corporation of America (MCA) and Gulf & Western. All of a sudden, he was the premier analyst covering this emerging sector.

All of these moguls liked him and would take his calls. After all, he was the only one who reached out to them when they were still struggling to build their empires.

Prestigious publications—*The New York Times*, *The Wall Street Journal*, *Barron's*—began calling him for his opinions on companies and marketing moves. He enjoyed this and did deep research and gave trenchant views in pithy language. The press adored him and came back to him for follow-up quotes.

The job he had once hated became one he loved and then became his calling.

My friend was candid and humble. He recognized the role that luck had played in his ascent, and he was grateful. Letting go of resistance is a part of that luck.

Here is a very powerful and instructive quotation from Rumi:

> When I run after what I think I want, my days are a furnace of stress and anxiety; if I sit in my own place of patience, what I need flows to me, and without pain. From this I understand that what I want also wants me, is looking for me and attracting me. There is a great secret here for anyone who can grasp it.*

And there is indeed a great secret in this concept. If you embrace this wisdom, you will be able to cut the mental and physical tethers that bind you to stress and free yourself to live a rich, sovereign life.

*Rumi, *Rumi Poetry: 100 Bedtime Verses*, Createspace Independent Pub, 2017.

8

IT MATTERS GREATLY WHERE YOU LIVE

If you are a real estate agent, you learn early on that the most important thing, the only thing that matters, is location, location, location!

Yes, it matters hugely where you live. Where you live determines how happy you are and whether there is meaning and joy in your life. And yet, most of us choose to live in hovels and surround ourselves with garbage. Even excrement.

Puzzled? Read on.

We don't live in a bungalow, duplex, mansion or an apartment. We live in our minds. Yes, that is our permanent residence—a place where there are no constraints of square footage. It's a vast space with unlimited area. We have the power to draw—and redraw—our boundaries as we see fit in order to create our ideal surroundings.

We don't live in a bungalow, duplex, mansion or an apartment. We live in our minds.

And you know what? No matter how grand our rooms, balconies, garages and verandas are, life is good only when things are clean and sorted there—in our mind. But that is where we keep things messy.

Regrets piled up in one corner, expectations stuffed in a

closet, secrets under the carpet, worries littered everywhere, comparisons spilled on the table, complexes leaking from bottles, grudges stinking in a box and anxieties in every room.

Be aware. This is our real home. And we cannot outsource the housekeeping. We have to do it ourselves. Take John, for instance.

John had a Harvard MBA and considered himself smarter than most of his peers. But life was not unfolding the way he thought it would.

He was passed over for promotion, and the company decided to bring in someone from the outside. The new person was also a Harvard MBA and a year his junior. He thought the person was incompetent, and seethed at the injustice.

He could have joined a startup venture capital firm but had turned it down because the hours were too long, his bonus was uncertain and he wanted stability. That firm now had multiple unicorns in its stable and was the lead investor in two of them. He regretted his decision every day.

He was worried about his son. The kid spent too much time playing tennis and not enough on schoolwork. He had decent grades, but 3.3 was not going to get him into the Ivies. And his tennis game was not good enough to get him an athletic scholarship.

He also brooded about his marriage. His wife was a teacher and a good homemaker, but she was just not 'right' for the circles he was entering into. His new boss, for example, was married to a stunner who also did billion-dollar deals for the private equity firm she worked for. She was likely to make partner this year.

Ten years ago, he would have been thrilled to live in the house he was in. Now it seemed drab and inferior. He wanted to entertain at home but was ashamed to invite his colleagues to his inadequate abode and have them meet his plain-Jane spouse, who was more likely to talk about children than art and culture.

His sense of dissatisfaction was growing stronger by the day.

Where exactly is John living?

It's certainly not a dwelling that radiates peace and calm. He has constructed his world with his mental chatter. He's experiencing it in precisely the way he built it. And he has no clue that this is what he has done. In fact, he's convinced that he's had bad breaks in his career path, choice of spouse and many other facets of his life.

There is a lesson here for you.

You are incredibly privileged. Your situation is significantly better than that of the vast majority of the world's population. You don't have to be concerned about whether you will have lunch tomorrow. You have a bed to sleep in and a roof over your head.

But you don't *feel* privileged.

You feel stressed and are painfully conscious of where you *could* have been and *should* have been, as well as where others are and you are not. This is because your mental chatter is running your life. It is designing the house you live in.

There is a simple solution for this.

Start observing your mental chatter and note how it takes you to places and then triggers the emotions you feel.

John's mental chatter led him to envy his boss and feel depressed about his lot in life—the very lot he dreamed about a decade ago. It is, of course, a capital idea to try to better oneself financially, materially, spiritually and every other way. It is a terrible idea to compare oneself to others, imagine the life you think they are leading and then feel miserable because you are not where you think they are.

Sadly, what irks John is that he is not living the kind of life he thinks others are living, and he would like to reach that imaginary place.

John has not examined the mental model he holds—one that requires his wife to be accepted by his aspirational group for him to feel proud of her. But does he truly want this? What would this do to the manner in which she presently runs his house and brings up his children?

John is certainly well off. Should he celebrate what he has or mourn what he does not have? The answer is painfully obvious.

Does this mean John should give up on his dreams?

Not at all.

We grow by expanding our horizons and striving to achieve our visions. But John can endeavour to progress in his career from a place of gratitude. He can be appreciative of where he is and what he has been able to achieve, and grateful for what will come tomorrow in his current company or elsewhere.

Instead, he has chosen to try and improve his lot from a place of deep dissatisfaction. And he does not realize that it was his choice. Probably it was an unconscious choice, but it was still a choice and still *his* choice.

He could be grateful that he has a loving partner who is also a good mother and devoted to making a haimish home. Or he could be driven by his fantasy of a trophy spouse and the advantages of being with her. Some fantasies are best not probed or indulged.

Again, it is a choice—and it is his choice.

When you observe your mental chatter, you quickly see that it takes you to places you would rather not visit. It is actually quite easy to turn it around, much as you would a horse you are riding. When envy raises its green head, direct your thoughts to how much you have to be grateful for.

And from that place of gratitude, try to do better.

Where are *you* living?

9

TURNING THE HORSE AROUND

Do you sometimes feel stuck in a rut? Do you work the same job, meet the same people, interact the same way with those same people and live a predictable life that has few surprises?

Here is how you can zhuzh up your life. Here is how you can make the world—or at least your neck of it—a better place. And the key to that is understanding that what you believe, determines where you live and where you can go.

I speak about mental models a lot because they are so central to our experience of life. Again, a mental model is a notion we have of the way the world works. We have dozens of them.

Do you believe that fat people are lazy and undisciplined? Do you believe that if they only ate less and exercised more, they would be healthier?

That is a mental model.

The problem is not that you have mental models—everyone has them. The problem is that you do not recognize that you have mental models.

The problem is that you do not recognize that you have mental models.

You think they are real and not

models. You believe they are such an accurate depiction of reality that you don't have to question them or give a second thought to them.

The vast majority of your mental models serve you well. That's why you have been able to accomplish all that you have. But some of your models do not serve you well—and those models are responsible for *all* the problems in your life.

I did not say *some* of your problems.

I said *all* your problems.

In part, this is to be provocative. I use this to carry the discussion to a deeper level with the clients I coach, and in the programmes and workshops I run.

But for our purposes here, let me share an exercise with you. It is designed to put some excitement in your life and bring a twinkle in your eye.

It will force you out of the narrow furrow in which you are travelling so that you can encounter—and create—stimulating new pathways.

Try it conscientiously for a month, and see how you feel. Start by thinking of someone in your life whom you dislike. Perhaps he or she has different political views or values you abhor or is slovenly, rude or totally selfish. It can be any quality that offends you and raises your hackles.

Can you actually get to like this person?

Abraham Lincoln supposedly said, 'I don't like that man. I must get to know him better.'

Try to use this mental model: '"I don't like him" means that I don't know him well enough.'

Look for traits in this person that you find likeable.

Find out what makes him tick as a human being. Note the ways in which you are similar—because we all have something in common, no matter how vastly different we are. Do you like the same series on Netflix? Root for the same tennis player? Enjoy solving advanced Sudoku puzzles? See how you feel about the person after you have done this. And note how you feel about yourself.

Excitement comes into your life when you change the way in which you view your daily activities, your career, your spouse and your children. This is more easily done than getting to the greener grass on the other side of an insurmountable fence.

Here is a powerful suggestion: Replace 'have to' with 'get to' in your life.

For instance, you don't *have to* feed your son breakfast and walk with him to the school bus. Instead, you *get to* feed him breakfast and walk with him to the school bus.

You don't *have to* go to work. You *get to* go to work—and perhaps, you should be grateful you have a job to go to when there are so many who don't.

You don't *have to* eat the healthy dinner you had the time and luxury to make, instead of choosing the easy option of grabbing your favourite carryout in its convenient Styrofoam packaging. You *get to* do this for yourself, as well as for others that may live in your household, so that you live a healthier life.

It seems simple, and it is. But it can make a profound change in how you experience life. It will certainly create a better home in which to live.

10

THE DIRT IS ON YOUR FACE—WHY DO YOU CLEAN THE MIRROR?

I conducted an independent project under Dr Kamla Chowdhry when I was at the Indian Institute of Management in Ahmedabad. She was a noted social psychologist and had a penetrating insight into the human psyche.

In my paper, I waxed indignant against persons who displayed a particular character trait. She summoned me to her office, which was crammed with books and papers and found a place for me to sit. I was nervous because she had a reputation as a tartar. I need not have worried. She asked me a series of gently probing questions until I realized that what I was railing against was also a problem in my own life—one that I resisted acknowledging.

We never see the world as it is—we see the world as we are.

We never see the world as it is—we see the world as we are.

Look around you at the persons in your life, and observe them closely. The persistent bore complains about how long-winded everyone is. The totally self-centered lout laments the selfishness of others. What we consistently observe about others says a great deal about us.

Patrick was penniless when he came to the United States (US). He joined a sweatshop and learned tailoring. He worked hard and soon saved enough money and garnered enough skill to open his own shop. He was ambitious and put in long hours. In a few years, his chain of upscale men's clothing stores made him a multimillionaire.

He finally took a vacation in Europe and held court to admiring relatives when he came back to the US.

'And when we went to Rome, I had a private audience with the pope,' he announced grandly. There was a collective sigh as the audience tried to assimilate this momentous news.

'Yep,' Patrick continued, savouring the situation, 'there was just the two of us in this huge office.'

There was more silence. Finally, an aunt ventured, 'Well, Patrick, how was he?'

'Size 38 long,' said Patrick promptly, 'but he's tough to outfit because his trousers are size 42.'

One of the participants in my live programme, a surgeon from Ohio, summarized it neatly: 'If you can spot it, you got it!'

What do you notice about persons you meet? Do you see that she is shabbily dressed or that there is genuine affection in her greeting? Do you make note that he went to an obscure no-name college or that he has a deep curiosity and knowledge about many disparate fields?

He was a good cat burglar, the best in the game.

He climbed in through the attic window, and his crepe-soled shoes made no noise as he moved through the house picking up valuable mementos and putting them noiselessly in a chamois bag.

The house belonged to a hedge fund mogul, and priceless objets d'art, such as Fabergé eggs, were everywhere.

But the thief had an enemy of sorts. Another thief who used similar techniques had already thwarted him by raiding two houses he had earmarked for a visit. Tonight, he was ready for anything. Though the house he walked through, silently collecting item after item, appeared untouched by any previous burglars, he kept his eyes open and there was a pistol in his pocket.

It was a bizarre, truth-is-stranger-than-fiction replay of the fifties romantic thriller *To Catch a Thief*.

And, exactly as in the movie, it turned out that his rival was also in the house. He sensed the presence and then saw him in a shadowy flicker.

He was glad that he had come prepared. He rose up suddenly, and so did his adversary. He raised his pistol and fired rapidly, aiming slightly left and centre, and slightly right to be sure of hitting his target.

There was a crash. The wall was a mirror and it shattered, and some of the glass fragments hit him.

It is ever thus in life. We fight with mirrors as we try to defend ourselves. Our enemy is within us. It is in our envy, hatred, sloth and our desperate need to be more, get more and be seen as more and better.

And because it is in us, we see it everywhere.

Why do we clean the mirror when the dirt is on our face?

Think about this.

11

END YOUR SLEEPLESS NIGHTS

What do you do when you go to bed and all you can do is toss and turn?

What can you do?

This is a global problem, and the question has come up again and again in the hundreds of talks I have given all over the world. It seems to be afflicting more and more people. It is likely that you, too, have suffered from it at some time. Or you will.

I remember an address I delivered at Warwick Business School in London—one of my favourite cities. The audience was engaged, and an earnest woman asked me for help.

She was going through a rough patch at work and thought she was in real danger of being pink-slipped. She said, 'When I go to bed, I just can't fall asleep. I've tried counting sheep. I've tried a glass of warm milk. I've tried vigorous exercise. They simply don't work for me.'

We all know that getting an adequate amount of sleep is essential for good health and optimal mental functioning. 'Adequate' may vary with individual and age, but at least seven hours sleep is a good benchmark.

So why do we fall short? Why do we toss and turn and

fall into a fitful slumber from which we emerge bleary-eyed and tired? And then we attempt to power our way through yet another day with caffeine imparted by coffee or colas. Some use stronger, and possibly illegal, substances.

The reason is your mental chatter. That incessant stream of insistent thought that is always with you, that paints dark scenarios of the future and forces you to dwell there.

You spend enormous amounts of your emotional energy contemplating the two or three things that are wrong in your life.

More precisely, you focus on the two or three things that you have arbitrarily decided are wrong with your life. And you completely ignore the 50 to 500 things that are pretty darn good about your life.

You feel put-upon and stressed out. This is because you let your mental chatter take you to areas of disturbance in life and expend your emotional energy there.

Your awareness is like a flashlight. A flashlight illuminates whatever you shine it on. Shine it on the ceiling, and it lights it up. Shine it on the floor, and that is what becomes bright and visible.

Your awareness is like a flashlight. A flashlight illuminates whatever you shine it on.

Starting tonight, try this: Shine the flashlight of your awareness on the many ways in which you are truly blessed and fortunate.

Five minutes before you go to bed, consciously think of how your life is unfolding exactly as you would wish in many areas.

Experience the feeling of gratitude. Feel it arise from the soles of your feet and well up through your body, and then gush out through your face.

This is not a 'thinking' exercise. You cannot make a checklist and go through it. Food to eat, check. Roof over head, check. Good health, check. You must actually *feel* the gratitude, not just think it.

A good way to move from thinking gratitude to feeling gratitude is to think about it mindfully and constantly. Repeatedly register in your mind that you are well and fortunate to have the problems you complain about. Don't wait for good weather—learn to dance in the rain.

If you persist, the thinking will turn to feeling and you will experience gratitude. There will be a lightness in you, and the world will seem rosier. Yes, there are problems you have to deal with, but you know you can handle them and that things will work out somehow.

Then go to bed.

Your sleepless nights will come to an end. Many of my students report that they began the exercise but never finished it because they fell asleep.

I hope that this will also become your problem.

12

THE STRANGE DISAPPEARANCE OF THE WEDDING GUEST

Great teachers frequently teach through parables. One such parable is that of the wedding guest who disappeared. It was actually a wedding crasher who vanished, but that term was not used in those days. Here is my version of this fable. It is more modern.

Corbett was a superior wedding crasher. He modestly believed that he was one of the very best.

Inferior wedding crashers would hang around at the periphery of the party and try to be inconspicuous.

Superior wedding crashers would maintain a brash presence and go up and kiss the bride, and wink at the bridegroom and give him tips on how to live a happy married life.

Corbett was casing a wedding he intended to crash shortly. He loved the excitement, the feeling of being on the edge, the thrill of outwitting those who were charged with keeping him and his ilk out.

The events register of the hotel listed 'Wedding

reception of Sandhya Mehta and Gerald Susskind'—and that was all he needed.

LinkedIn told him that the groom was an investment banker, and the bride was a public-relations executive. It was an intercultural marriage.

Once he arrived at the scene, he observed that the gatekeepers looked at the invitation cards before letting guests in, but their glance was cursory.

This would be pie.

In tougher weddings, the guards examined invitation cards closely and then matched each against a list of invited guests. In still more exclusive events, the sentries used biometric identification before permitting entry. Security methods included retinal scans and fingerprints and, on one occasion, voice identification.

Corbett had crashed them all.

He had developed ingenious ways of bypassing identification barriers. At this particular event, he noticed that most men received their invitations back and put them in the side pocket of their jackets.

He strolled casually into the men's room and waited, washing his hands numerous times. Soon, a well-scrubbed young man appeared with the edge of his invitation peeking out of his side pocket.

Corbett straightened up, stumbled and bumped heavily into the newcomer. 'I'm so sorry,' he apologized. 'Are you okay?' He patted him in a friendly manner, and picked up the invitation.

Ten minutes later, he was at the reception sipping a cocktail. He surveyed the guests, noting who was chatting with whom. He was good at reading body language.

He could easily determine who was important and who merely thought they were important.

He picked up a label from the table by the entrance and wrote a bold Corbett on it with curves and curlicues. He affixed it to his jacket lapel. He was wearing a colourful tie. There was no way anyone could miss it. He wanted to be noticed and remembered.

He made his way to the throng around the bride, cut in effortlessly and gave her a big hug. He kissed her on the cheek, and it was not a perfunctory kiss.

'You are the most beautiful woman he was ever engaged to,' he whispered in her ear. 'For the longest time, he thought you were "not good enough". I am so glad you were able to get him to change his mind.'

Her head jerked up sharply, and he gave her an affectionate smile and slipped away.

A heavyset woman came toward him, brushing aside the guests in her path like the prow of a battleship scattering fishing boats. The mother of the bride, he guessed. He had seen them confabulating.

He turned and smiled at her before she could accost him. 'I'm with Grey Financial,' he volunteered, naming the company that Gerald worked for. 'We are involved in a major deal, and I could only slip away for a few minutes. I will have to leave shortly.'

The battleship relaxed. Obviously, a friend of her son-in-law. Perhaps even his boss. Best to keep him in good humour.

She asked him solicitously if he had eaten.

He assured her that he had, and she walked away.

It was really simple. First, you found out whether the

person you were speaking to was part of the bride's family or the groom's family. And then you positioned yourself as part of the extended family of the other. Or a friend of the other.

'And you are…?' inquired an elderly gentleman. He was trim and bald, but he had tufts of neatly groomed white hair.

'I'm Corbett,' he said, heartily pumping the other's hand. 'And you are…?'

The man ignored his query. 'Sandhya asked me to find out who you were,' he said brusquely.

Girl's family, thought Corbett and promptly put himself on the other side. 'I went to school with Gerald,' he explained.

'I am Gerald's father, and I know all his school friends,' said the other suspiciously. 'I don't recall seeing you before.'

Oops! Major blooper. Time to shift gears

'You caught me out,' he said admiringly—and also placatingly. 'I don't know either Sandhya or Gerald. I am actually the representative of the Wedding Gift company. A major gift is arriving in thirty minutes, and I will demonstrate it.'

Corbett looked searchingly at the other's face and saw the lines relax. He pressed his advantage home. 'Nobody knows about it,' he continued. 'Now you do, but please keep it secret. It is intended to be a surprise.'

The old man smiled broadly and winked. 'Mum's the word,' he said, placing a finger across his lips.

Corbett moved to the buffet table and heaped his plate. The food was good, so he took seconds. He then slowly approached the bridegroom, who was talking to a group. He waited till Gerald was temporarily alone and then congratulated him. 'You really are a lucky man,' he gushed. 'Sandhya truly wanted to marry Roger after their weekend fling, but he just would not commit. I am so happy you were there for her rebound.'

'Excuse me?' Gerald exclaimed, but the others had come back and Corbett had already moved away.

What a fun reception this was! Corbett was enjoying himself thoroughly. He helped himself to a cocktail. And then another.

He caught a slight commotion out of the corner of his eye and noticed a huddle. The huddle broke, and a group of four started moving determinedly toward him. It was the bride, the battleship, the groom and his father.

Time to leave.

A waiter was passing by with a full tray at shoulder height. Corbett tripped him adroitly, and pandemonium reigned. He slipped out quietly and reached home a half hour later. It had been a good evening.

There is a wedding guest—or wedding crasher—in your life, and it is busy screwing up your life. This crasher is your mind, and it is constantly directing your attention elsewhere and outside.

Your mind is like an untrained stallion that takes you where it wants to go.

Like Corbett, it plants worry and dissension.

The mind is simply an unceasing flow of thoughts, and they are all directed outward. It's like an untrained stallion that takes you where it wants to go. When you begin to observe it and inquire into its nature, it subsides. It may even disappear, like Corbett. And that is the start of your spiritual journey.

13

THE TERRIBLE MISTAKE YOU MAKE EVERY DAY

There is a habit that keeps you from reaching the heights of which you are capable. It has hampered you all your life, and its influence has been all the more pernicious because you did not even recognize it.

Pedro was rushing to his office. He was late and was slated for an important part of a presentation. He also suspected that, behind his back, his colleagues wanted him to trip. His thoughts were raging as he navigated the heavy pedestrian traffic.

'I've done it again. Why do I never get these simple things right? I meant to get to the conference room 15 minutes early so I had plenty of time to set up, and now I may not even make it in time to start when called on.

'Good thing I sent my slides over yesterday. What do I do if they have not been loaded? I should have checked with Pam about this. Why do I always screw up like this? I bet the others think I'm the "token" minority and are sniggering at all the foolish mistakes I make. I think I am as good as any of them, but if I keep fouling up like this I'll never get a chance to prove it. After all, how tough is it to set my iPhone reminder to go off 15 minutes earlier?'

Pedro has an internal voice telling him off. And you have one too!

How many times has this voice told you that you are not good enough? That someone else is way better than you in intelligence, athletic ability, physical attractiveness and earning potential? That you will never be able to do as well as someone you know?

We talk to ourselves all the time. Much of the time, we run ourselves down. We compare ourselves unfavourably to others. We pass judgement on what we perceive as our major faults without hesitation. We criticize our appearance, our performance, our ability to maintain relationships, our station in life and our various character traits. Maybe we are too shy, not funny enough or we always overeat

We are mentally slashing our wrists every day.

We are mentally slashing our wrists every day. And we do not realize how much this habit is hampering us. It prevents us from being happy. It keeps us from even beginning to realize our potential.

It is our single worst enemy.

This is the foe that frequently disparages us and points out our many failings. It is an adversary we all have. Here is a typical example: 'I know I should not have had that second slice of pizza, but I did it anyway. I have no willpower. That's why I'll never amount to anything. Why can't I ever stick to a decision?'

All of us have that internal monologue. But there is

something you can do about this. You cannot slay this enemy, but you can effectively tie him up when you understand that the mistake you make is that you *believe* the enemy.

You think this voice is you and that it is true. But even a cursory examination of your own experience will show you how wrong this mental chatter can be. You are expecting a call from an important client, and the call does not come. You immediately think, *He is unhappy. I know he is unhappy. I should have given him that extra discount on his last order. He has been talking to another supplier. What can I do to make things right?*

And then, it turns out that the client has some perfectly innocent reason for missing the call, such as a dental emergency or something even simpler—like he just forgot. And no, he is not considering defecting.

One of my students is the mother of a hearing-impaired son. Every time he takes a trip and does not call in to let her know he's arrived safely, she frets with visions of plane crashes, fainting fits and other unnamed disasters. Decades of her son making safe, uneventful journeys have not cured her.

How often has *your* voice been wrong? If you do a careful analysis, you will be astonished at how many times it has misled you.

Despite this, you believe it and identify with it.

So, the next time your inner voice tries to take you to a dark place, pause immediately. Recognize that it is just a voice in your head. It is *not* an oracle, and it is not necessarily truthful. Most of all, it is *not* you.

It is just a voice in your head.

Observe it as if it were a movie and you are the audience.

If you can do this, you will discover that your mental chatter does not like being viewed. Its intensity diminishes, and its tenor changes.

And soon enough, you don't go to those dark places anymore.

Just being aware of your mental chatter begins to liberate you from the prison you have constructed, and in which you live.

14

KILL THAT CHILD! YOUR LIFE DEPENDS ON IT!

When I was young, I went to a Jesuit school. We began each day with the Lord's prayer, and the first class was 'Morals'. We were issued an illustrated book for that class, and it was full of stories. I vividly remember that I found the one that had some pictures somewhat frightening as a child.

The tale was about a king who used to ride alone to clear his head. One day a small child accosted him and tried to stab him with a play sword. The king, touched by the boy's playful and fearless spirit, came down from his horse, laughingly brushed aside the weapon and kissed the child.

The next day, the child appeared again, a little bigger and stronger and the scenario repeated itself. The king laughed.

Each day, the boy grew in size and his sword grew in heft. The king protected himself easily and spared his opponent. He quite enjoyed this diversion during his solitary rides.

The boy became a young man and now wielded a tempered blade. There came a day when the king had to expend all his skill and strength to parry his strokes, and was wounded when he finally subdued his adversary. The king was angry now, but the young man cried piteously so the king sheathed his sword and spared his life.

The following day, the muscular man jumped from a tree and knocked the king from his horse. In a flash, the man disarmed the monarch and bound his hands.

The king was bemused and complacent. 'Okay, you finally won,' he said. 'Tomorrow will be a different story.'

'There will be no tomorrow,' the man said sourly as he lopped off the king's head.

A somewhat gruesome story for a seven-year-old, but the lesson it conveyed was powerful. We have many destructive tendencies and addictions. They all begin with a vague and comforting desire, like the tendrils of some tropical plant. You tell yourself, *I'll have one more cigarette because it feels so good, and I need it to calm my nerves. One more drink to relax after this horrible day.*

Surely one cigarette, one drink, one serving of junk food or one of whatever won't hurt?

And that is where you begin your destructive slide. One will not hurt. But many ones piled on top of each other become devastating. The tendril becomes a thick cord that can strangle you. The small child becomes a man and decapitates you.

> *You did not become fat with a single bite or a single meal.*

You did not become fat with a single bite or a single meal. Your life did not stagnate because of a single ill-spent day. Recognize the child that, when grown up, can raze your dreams.

Odds are that your foe is not a child anymore. But he is still weaker than you. Kill him right now. If you don't take immediate action, regret will inevitably follow.

The language is horrific, but the message is not. You need to do this if you want peace.

15

MAKING A QUANTUM LEAP

Many persons who apply for my programmes or approach me for personal coaching feel stuck. They think they should be ahead of where they are and are frustrated at how slowly they are advancing.

It is possible for them to leapfrog several levels of accomplishment. And do it again. And again. You can do this also. I will show you how you can achieve this in every area of your life.

There is a secret to reaching new heights in your personal journey. Let's begin with Susan's experience.

> Susan was steaming. She had been serving as the interim chief marketing officer of a large electronics company and was on the committee searching for a permanent hire.
>
> She had thrown her own hat in the ring and was the internal candidate. She had been with the company for five years, received stellar reviews and thought she was well-liked.
>
> She was highly qualified with a bachelor's degree in science from Harvard and an MBA from Columbia Business School.

David was the final choice. He also had a science background and an MBA from Columbia. He had graduated three years after her and was four years younger.

Everyone thought he was smart—an up-and-comer who would go places fast.

Susan agreed. She just thought that she was too, she had more experience and was the better candidate. She didn't know why she had not coasted into the job as the first choice. She was unsure whether her gender had worked against her, and this bothered her.

She was angry and considered quitting.

Something like this has happened to you. Or it will. Someone younger and seemingly less qualified will zoom past you in some area that is important to you. What should you do? What *can* you do?

The answer comes at different levels.

First, it is extraordinarily foolish—and toxic—to measure yourself against someone else and let this measurement determine your well-being.

Second, there are steps you can take to jump ahead in your own career. Let's talk about this. Many people believe that success comes from patient hard work and climbing the ladder of success step-by-step.

I disagree.

You can jump ahead to the next queue and then move to the head of the one after that. You cannot achieve such spurts by *working harder*. In fact, working harder may actually set you back.

You cannot do it by working smarter. In these days of connection and information, everyone is privy to the same knowledge sources. You cannot do it by *managing your time better*. This is a seductive notion, but you will be dismayed at how much time you spend in an effort to manage that time.

The only way you can achieve such jumps in your life is by *thinking differently*—by thinking radically differently.

This is not a new concept. Everyone knows it at some level, and you have been exposed to the idea many times in your life.

You have been told to 'see the glass as half full, not half empty' and that 'every problem is an opportunity in disguise' and you know that 'when the going gets tough, the tough get going'.

But despite this knowledge, the vast majority find it difficult to 'think differently'. Why? Because you *cannot* think differently by *trying* to think differently.

You cannot think differently by *trying* to think differently.

The only way you can consistently think differently is by examining the mental models that cause you to think the way you do, and then making changes in them. For some models, there will be small tweaks. For other models, you will have to do some major restructuring. But when you are done, you will see the world differently. To many around you, your thinking will seem radically different. To you, this different mode of thinking will become natural.

Here is an example of what I mean.

I grew up in India, in a middle-class family. My father was a government bureaucrat, and my mother was a homemaker. We were not poor, but there wasn't a lot of discretionary cash lying around.

One evening, we were walking near an open-air market in Karol Bagh (a section of Delhi) when I was approached by a vendor selling assorted knick-knacks from a wooden shelf strapped in front of his stomach.

One item was a book called *Just Like Daddy*, and I was taken by it.

The cover was blue, and it had pictures. It was about a boy who got up in the morning and brushed his teeth just like daddy, and did other things just like his father did. It was actually two books, because if you flipped it around, it turned pink and had a little girl who did things just like mommy.

For some reason I cannot now fathom, I really, really wanted that book. I put in a petition, and my parents looked at it.

It had only a few words on each page, and I was already reading junior classics so my petition was denied.

We walked on. The vendor followed behind. Every time I looked back, he flashed the book at me. He seemed to have a childlike faith in my ability to swing the deal and was eager for me to do so. Perhaps his children's dinner depended on my success.

My mother was a frugal lady who hardly ever bought anything for herself, but on this occasion she saw a purse she liked and reached for it.

I saw my opportunity and dove into it like a trained seal.

With tears rolling down my cheeks, I bawled loudly and asked how she could possibly buy something so utterly useless as a purse while there was this great educational material they were denying me.

It was a low blow.

It worked.

Back went the purse, and I got *Just Like Daddy*. I was pleased as punch, and there was a distinct coolness between my parents and me for a while.

I mention this story because a couple of decades later I saw *Just Like Daddy* at a flea market.

All the memories came flooding back.

But there was a difference.

I clearly remembered all that had happened, but *Just Like Daddy* no longer had any hold on me.

I did not want it. I did not *not* want it.

It was irrelevant to my life. I had outgrown my need for *Just Like Daddy.*

Look back on your life. You will recall many things that, at some point, you desperately wanted. You may have gotten them. Or you may not have gotten them.

It does not matter.

What matters is that you no longer have a need for them.

They are irrelevant to your life now. You have outgrown them.

Right now, in your life, there is something you want a great deal. It is creating turmoil in your life because you do not have it. Perhaps you want your bank to extend your credit line so that you can use the funds to expand your business. Or you would like your daughter to shape up and improve her grades. Or your company to make the 'Best Place to Work' List. Or your in-laws to move to Australia.

There is something you want, and you don't have it and it is causing you angst. Here is my question for you: Would you rather get what you want? Or would you rather outgrow your need for it, as I outgrew my need for *Just Like Daddy* and you outgrew your need for countless things in the past?

Imagine that you have vaulted to levels so much higher than where you are, that you no longer have the need for the experience you are seeking.

What would your life be like?

Think about it.

It's a good illustration of what I mean when I exhort you to think differently. Here is an exercise you can do right away to get you started on thinking differently. Pick anything going on in your life right now that is soaking up a lot of emotional energy—something you see as a 'bad thing' or even a 'very bad thing'.

Is there any scenario you can visualize by which this could turn out to be a 'good thing' in a few months or years? And then ask yourself if there is anything you can proactively do to *make* it a good thing. Asking this question and taking such action, moves you from the realm of despair to the realm of possibility. It makes you resilient—so resilient that others wonder how you do it.

One of my students was laid off from a large technology company with a reputation for not firing its workers. It was a major shock. His wife was a homemaker, and he had four children.

The company did not want a reputational hit, so he got a handsome severance package. He used it to start a business that prospered mightily and more than doubled his income within two years.

Many who have taken my Creativity and Personal Mastery programme say it has changed so many of their mental models that it has made them new persons. And, of course, these new persons naturally think differently.

The change that happens within you lets you experience life ever so differently and joyously. It helps you reach heights you never dreamed possible, even as the sense of effort and strain leave you.

And that brings us back to Susan, whom we left smarting because she was passed over for a position for which she felt she was eminently qualified. She spent a week or so crying her heart out and then resolved to make David her ally and advocate. This was surprisingly easy once she set her mind to it. They had gone to the same business school, studied with the same professors and had many friends in common. They got along famously.

Eighteen months later, David came to her with an idea he had. She thought it was brilliant, and both of them quit to start their own company.

Always bear the following in mind: Fate does not give you a lemon, and you do not have to think you must make the best of this and make lemonade out of it.

Oh, no! That is not how it is.

Fate gives you the opportunity to make lemonade, and if you are smart you will streamline the process and create a global empire of lemonade stands.

That is exactly what Ray Kroc did with burgers.

16

IT WAS NEVER ABOUT YOU

I once wrote a blog post in which I shared the story of one of my students who worked for a large technology company and was chafing at the corporate collar. My course had opened him up to boundless possibilities, and he wanted out. His only concern was that he lacked the finances to fund his startup.

The company was restructuring and offered a generous package to those who chose to leave. He was a valued team member and not expected to depart, but he grabbed the opportunity with both hands. The severance bankrolled his new venture, which succeeded spectacularly. Soon, he was making twice of what he had been making at his previous job.

> *When you begin to think differently, you become a different person and the world changes. You experience life in an entirely new manner.*

The student read my post and got back in touch with me. It turns out that, in five years, the income replacement shot up to five times his previous salary. He had been meaning to thank me, and my blog was the reminder he needed to reach out.

That is how the universe works!

When you begin to *think* differently, you *become* a different person and the world changes. You experience life in an entirely new manner. The universe becomes more friendly and works to help you get what you want.

This works even better if you let go of strong 'wants' and leave it to the universe to decide what comes your way. Let me give you a personal example of how I learned to think differently. It may also help you.

Growing up in India and Burma (now Myanmar), I learnt English and built up my vocabulary by reading. I knew the words, but I did not always know how to pronounce them in context.

And English, in case you haven't noticed, is idiosyncratic.

Thus, you would like to 'read' a book but have 'r-e-d' it after you are done. And let's not even talk about Leicester Square and Gloucestershire.

My publisher wanted me to narrate the audio version of my book, *Are YOU Ready to Succeed?* I was teaching at London Business School at the time, so they rented a studio in London and hired a freelance BBC producer to manage the project.

She was an honest-to-goodness dame—very polished, polite and professional. I was in a sound booth with microphones so sensitive that there was a mesh screen between it and my face, so my breathing did not get recorded.

The producer was endlessly patient as she said, 'Srikumar, let's try it like *this*,' over and over and over. My ears burned as I realized how many words I mispronounced and how often I laid the accent on the wrong syllable. When the ordeal was done, I swore I would hire an elocution coach and work with him for six months.

I did not.

Shortly thereafter, I wished I had followed through on my intention. I was speaking to an audience of 500 executives of a large financial services firm and said something they did not understand.

It was important, so someone from the audience interrupted and asked me what I had just said. I repeated it.

They still did not understand.

Then someone from the audience chimed in. 'I think he means…' The entire audience burst out laughing. Loud, rib-tickling, belly-busting laughs. If possible, I would have sunk through the floor and pulled it in after me.

Later, a veteran speaker gave me sage counsel.

'Srikumar,' he said, 'when you are onstage, the audience takes its cue from you. Stuff happens all the time. The microphone dies. Your PowerPoint slides get mixed up. Your video clips do not play. If you get rattled, they get rattled. But if you keep your cool, so will they and they will be grateful to you for it.'

'They laughed at me,' I stuttered.

'So?' he queried.

Then he said something I've never forgotten.

'Look, all of them are in high-pressure jobs. The company is restructuring and they are not sure where they will be next month or even if they will be able to keep their jobs. They are anxious and tense. You made them laugh uproariously and forget their concerns for a while. Be grateful you could do that.'

I thought about his words and changed my thinking. I am no longer concerned about what the audience thinks of me. I have no plans to hire an elocution coach. I focus entirely on how I can help them through the concepts I share, and these are truly life-changing.

My audience senses this and are patient, grateful and forgiving.

If I make an egregious mistake in pronunciation or grammar and they laugh, I laugh with them and am grateful to have brought some temporary joy into their lives.

They understand this and laugh with me rather than *at* me.

This approach has completely driven away my fear of public speaking.

I have a suggestion on 'thinking differently' that I would like to offer you: The next time you are called on to give a speech or need to have a serious conversation about an important matter, don't put your emotional energy into 'What will they think of me?' or 'What do I want to get out of this?'

Don't get me wrong. I am *not* saying that you should not be clear about what you would like to accomplish.

I *am* saying that you do not want to put your intensity into what you want. Put it into 'What can I do to help this person—or this audience—achieve their goals?'

See how you feel when you do this. I am willing to wager that your tension drops away. I think you'll find that you 'succeed' more often by thinking about how you can help, rather than by struggling to get what you want. Thinking differently brings changes in you and opportunities you could never have imagined.

One final note: Don't treat this as a sophisticated method of self-serving. By that, I mean try to avoid thinking along lines like, 'If I help him get what he wants, he will give me what I want.' Such an approach transforms whatever you do into a transaction and impoverishes you.

What you need will come to you organically from the universe. Be of service for one reason only—because you can be of service, and this brings joy into your life and makes the world a better place.

17

FEED THE DOG, NOT THE WOLF!

Remember this parable if you want to improve your life—and the world. And yes, there are many versions of the story, but I like this one. It comes from the Native American tradition.

> A young lad was about to take his place among the adults of the tribe, and the final step was an interview with the medicine man.
>
> 'Here is a dog,' said the medicine man. 'It is intelligent, loving, kind and trustworthy.'
>
> 'And here is a wolf—malevolent, vicious, cruel and ready to kill,' he continued. 'The dog and the wolf are fighting, and they are both inside you.'
>
> 'Which one will win?' asked the lad anxiously.
>
> 'Whichever one you feed,' said the medicine man gravely.

It is an intrinsically simple, yet an immensely instructive parable. Inside each of us are 'let's help one another and make the world a better place' impulses. We also have 'let me grab whatever I can for myself, and the Devil take the hindmost' impulses.

These two impulses are consistently and endlessly warring.

It is your job to identify and feed the dog in you. It is also your job to identify and selectively feed the dog in every person you meet—which, yes, is absolutely possible! Magic happens in your life when the dog in you becomes friends with the dog in another person.

It also often happens that we feed the wolf in us and in those we meet without even recognizing that we are doing so. Say, you meet a friend who is depressed at the state of the world. He rails against feckless politicians, crooked businesspersons and the increasing divisions in society. You commiserate with him and launch your diatribe against environmental despoliation, corrupt legislators and ineffective government.

In every interaction you have—with friends, spouses, children, colleagues or business associates—ask yourself, Am I feeding the dog, or am I feeding the wolf?

When you part, you feel warm about the camaraderie you've shared but you are oblivious that you have fed the wolf in both yourself and your friend.

Imagine if you had instead said, 'I entirely agree with you. But is there any sign that things are moving toward greater amity and cooperation? And is there anything we can do to foster movement in that direction?' If you approach the conversation in this way, you will have started to feed the dog.

So, in every interaction you have—with friends, spouses, children, colleagues or business associates—ask yourself, *Am I feeding the dog, or am I feeding the wolf?*

Are you bringing out the best in the person you are speaking to and leaving them energized with possibility and determined to do the same for others? Or are you leaving them more desolate and feeling down?

As you consciously practice this, your life becomes richer

and so does the lives of persons in your circle. Everybody wins. If everybody did likewise, the outside world would transform from a place of quiet desperation to a haven of radiant joy.

18

LET GO OF YOUR GRUDGES

What do you do if you have a spill on your countertop?
You clean it up.

You do have a mess on the figurative countertop of your mind, and it is spoiling your beautiful kitchen and your ability to cook healthy meals!

What I am about to share with you has no boundaries. It cuts across cultures, languages, religions and ethnic identities. I witnessed this phenomenon while I was teaching at London Business School, where my average class would have representatives from 20 or more countries.

Charlotte is a good example.

I had a dozen or more small-group exercises in my course and was forming the groups. Charlotte gently protested being in the same group as Shelley. 'She is thoughtless and rude,' she said. 'I don't think she should be in the class at all.'

I probed deeper.

It turned out that they had gone to the same school and had lost touch for years before they found themselves back together in the same business school. Decades earlier, in second or third grade, a group of girls had laughed at a colourful pinafore Charlotte had worn to school. Shelley was among them.

I probed deeper.

No, they had not interacted since school. They had not spoken to one another once during business school.

Charlotte, by now somewhat embarrassed by her comments, acknowledged that she was being guided by an ancient memory and perhaps needed a course correction.

But we are all Charlotte, at one point or another, and some of us on a daily basis.

Look at any interaction you have with a person who is an ongoing part of your life. Do you have an expectation of how this will go based on your previous meetings? More precisely, on the basis of your interpretation of your past conversations?

Recognize that it is not what happened in the past but what you think happened in the past that is colouring your expectation.

Look at the grudges you hold. They may be small. You may think them insignificant. But each is a silken thread, and many of them can bind you down.

How do you let go of the grudges you hold?

First, be aware of them.

When you meet someone with whom you have a troubled history, see clearly that what happened in the past is colouring your expectation of what will happen now and in the future. Recognize that it is not what happened in the past but what you *think* happened in the past that is colouring your expectation.

Then play a game.

Imagine that this is the first time you are meeting this person, and be open to whatever happens. Focus only on the way you are interacting in this fresh, new moment. Put your suitcases down! The train can carry you *and* your baggage.

Consciously determine that you will feed the dog.

Be prepared to be pleasantly surprised.

19

ARE YOU THE HUNGRY GHOST?

Creativity and Personal Mastery, the course I created, has been among the most popular and highest rated at many of the world's top business schools.

I learned a great deal from the highly intelligent and fiercely driven men and women who participated in my course and shared freely about the problems they were facing. I remember one whose tale touched many. Let's call him Joe.

> Joe was an immigrant and had some cultural issues, so he thought he did not 'fit in' with others. He was bright, but his accent was noticeable and probably contributed to his low self-esteem. He compensated by working really hard and this led to his staying ahead of most of his peers in salary and position. He felt CPM had authentically transformed his life and, for the first time, he started feeling at peace with himself and okay with whatever the future would bring.
>
> He had a young son, Adam—about eight at the time—and was also going through a somewhat contentious divorce. His soon-to-be ex-wife was planning to move to a different country, and they were working

out custody arrangements. His son was frequently silent and withdrawn, and Joe wanted to teach the lad the CPM exercises he had found so useful for himself.

One day, when the two of them were alone, he noticed his son's lip trembling. His wife had just stalked out of the house after a minor disagreement had escalated into a shouting match.

He hugged Adam and asked him how he was feeling. Adam burst out crying. He hated it when his parents fought, and he didn't like the thought of leaving his school and moving away to a different country.

Seeing an opening, Joe suggested that they play a game. 'You know, moving to a different country does not have to be challenging. Let's think of all the ways it might be fun.'

Adam was diffident but agreed to play. Soon, they were topping each other with ideas. Adam loved flying, and he would be doing lots of it as he went from parent to parent. He would have different toys in each of his homes, and different friends. He would be in a city with his father and in the country with his mother, and each had its charms. He would be able to bicycle to school when with his mother and stay up late when he visited his father.

Adam's eyes started shining, and he squealed with laughter as he listed the possibilities.

That really worked, thought Joe as the momentum eased. Tenderly, he asked Adam what else he could do for him.

Adam deflated visibly.

'I wish you would talk to me like you just did,' his son said. 'You are never there most of the time.'

Joe realized the truth of that statement like a blow to his solar plexus. Yes, he did try to be there for his son and take him to movies and come home for dinner. But he was always preoccupied—with his studies, with his job, with the deteriorating relationship with his wife.

As he shared this with the class, he wept for Adam's childhood that he had already missed. There was such heartfelt pathos in Joe's voice as he spoke about his realization that many in the class broke down and cried, and others had moist eyes.

Now, think of *your* life. Think of the time you spend with your partner and children and loved ones.

Are you really there? Or are you a hungry ghost going through the motions, obsessed with your mental chatter and driven by your needs? I will wager that you are more frequently the latter than you would like to be.

Are you really there? Or are you a hungry ghost going through the motions, obsessed with your mental chatter and driven by your needs?

Take heart. Don't beat yourself up.

For the moment, bring yourself to the present. Bring yourself to the person you are with. Pour your full, undivided attention into your interaction with that person. Do this especially with the important people in your life.

Also pay attention to the interactions happening inside your own head. Practice mindfulness. This will help you weed out the mental chatter, enjoy yourself in the present and be there for those you love. Your life will improve greatly if you practise this regularly.

20

GRATITUDE, EVERY DAY

We all have days that begin badly and then spiral downward, with more and more stuff going horribly wrong. What do you do when this is not one day but every day? When your whole life seems offtrack?

I read a moving, sad-funny-inspirational account of someone who dealt with this dilemma—who hit rock bottom and then bounced back. Of course, the depth that he reached does not compare to the real destitution one may experience daily in a developing country, but let's let that pass for now. There is a lesson here for all of us.

> He was a 52-year-old attorney whose practice was floundering. Thirty years after graduating from a prestigious law school, he was having difficulty making ends meet. His clients were not paying what they owed. And they were not dream clients who were a pleasure to work with—he scrambled for work and took what he got.
>
> He was forced to move to a dingy apartment where the air-conditioning barely worked. Inside, it felt like a sauna or a deep freeze, depending on the season. His second wife lived in the house he moved out of, and he

couldn't afford the alimony or child support. He could barely make payroll. One of his clients was suing him. It was a frivolous suit, but he still had to hire an attorney to defend himself and that was more cash out the door.

He met a wonderful woman whom he started to like, but she broke up with him shortly before Christmas. He looked at his collections and disbursements and realized that, after subtracting rent, payroll and other expenses, he had been working 60-plus hours a week for the whole year for nothing. He was also obese and unhealthy.

On a whim, he started to do something he had thought about for a long time but never implemented. His life began to change immediately. Within a year he experienced financial gain, weight loss, true friendship and inner peace.

Are you curious about what he did and whether this could work for you? You can read this man's full account in John Kralik's *365 Thank Yous: The Year a Simple Act of Daily Gratitude Changed My Life.*[*]

Each day, Kralik wrote a thoughtful, sincere thank-you note to someone who had affected him in some way. These were handwritten—not emails or texts—and he put much care into the wording. They were heartfelt.

When you start focussing on appreciating what others have done for you, there is a sharp decrease in lamentation about your own sorry state.

Telling you exactly how he turned his life around would be a spoiler, so I will desist from sharing. But I will say that the

---

[*] Kralik, John, *365 Thank Yous: The Year a Simple Act of Daily Gratitude Changed My Life*, Hyperion, 2010.

underlying theme of his journey and efforts is a core part of all my programmes. When you start focussing on appreciating what others have done for you, there is a sharp decrease in lamentation about your own sorry state.

When you move from bemoaning your misfortune to recognizing the goodness of others, you begin to occupy a different emotional domain—and your life blossoms.

And this is the key: The universe responds automatically and quickly to accommodate the new person you are becoming. You cannot be depressed when you are being appreciative, and expressing this sincerely.

I've said it before: We spend way too much time railing about the two or three things that we think are 'wrong' in our lives, and we ignore the 50 to 500 things that are pretty darn good.

Flip this around. Before you go to bed, consciously feel grateful for the many good things in your life. This is not an intellectual exercise, so you are not allowed to *think* gratitude. You actually have to feel it.

And then, when you wake up, do it again instead of immediately rushing to the space of 'there is too much to do and I don't have time to do it all'.

The way to truly feel gratitude is to constantly think about how much you have to be grateful for. Do this mindfully. Set alarms and reminders for yourself. Keep doing this, and one day you will discover that inner glow that tells you that a thought has become a felt experience.

See what a huge difference this makes in your life.

21

WHEN THE WORLD TURNS BLEAK

One cold day in Long Island, icy rain had turned my driveway slick. My wife refused to let me go out to pick up the newspaper. This was understandable, as her arm was in a cast. She had broken her left wrist after slipping on some ice two weeks before—and she felt one injured person in the family was quite enough.

Earlier that day, I had been watching CNN and the news was grim. President Obama had announced that he was considering sending lethal weapons to the Ukraine. The talking heads felt the situation would almost certainly escalate.

A week before that, I was at a party where the conversation turned to the terrible fate that had befallen the Jordanian pilot captured by ISIS. Feelings ran high, and desires for dramatic revenge were freely expressed.

What can you do when the world seems headed into a black hole, the weather is dreary and your work is not progressing in the way you think it should?

My situation on that day is a perfect example of how our thoughts and emotions are captured by external stimuli. We begin spiralling down and are in despair before we recognize what has happened.

When this happens to you, *pause*. Take several deep breaths. Bring your attention to your breath—going in, going out. Going in, going out.

Notice that what is troubling you is a thought. Maybe many thoughts, but they are just that—thoughts. If you can see that they are thoughts, then you become the observer of the thoughts and they cannot drag you along with them into a journey you do not wish to take.

Yes, terrible things are happening in the world today. But focussing on them and how terrible they are actually feeds the demonic energy that has been unleashed.

You cannot turn your back on horrible events, but neither should you be obsessed with them.

So, in your own small way, in your own small world, do what you can to help someone you know elevate his or her consciousness. Practise random acts of kindness. Remember that tyrants appear—and for a moment seem invincible—but eventually they fall.

In your own small way, in your own small world, do what you can to help someone you know elevate his or her consciousness. Practise random acts of kindness.

The occurrences that you find so troubling, the disappointments that are so galling, will fade in importance. When I was a doctoral student at Columbia Business School, the library went digital. In those days that meant microfiche and microfilm. I took a stack of discarded issues of *Fortune* magazine to my class. Every cover had a picture of the CEO of a major company. This person held sway over thousands of people. Sometimes he—the vast majority were male—could shake an entire industry or even the economy.

Most of my students could not recognize those one-time titans of industry. You can read Percy Bysshe Shelley's

'Ozymandias' for a poetic perspective.

Life is a passing show, so do not let temporary disturbances affect your equanimity.

Resolve that you—and only you—will control how you feel and that you will *not* let news anchors or external stimuli hijack your well-being.

Here is a tale that is not in the Mahabharata, the massive opus that is a big part of the cultural heritage of India. But it very well might have been because that work is replete with similar stories.

Arjuna, the third brother of the Pandava clan, was a great archer. He was reputedly the best in the world. He used his bow, Gandiva, so dexterously that he could shoot an arrow and then hit it with a second arrow before it had finished its flight.

Once, he was walking by himself and went farther than he intended. He came to a village where there were signs of an extraordinary bowman. There were painted targets everywhere—on the boles of trees, on the sides of barns and hanging on poles in the middle of fields.

And there was an arrow spang in the centre of every one of them. It was always in the bullseye, and many bullseyes were so tiny that the arrowhead was larger.

Arjuna noted one target that was wrapped around the corner of a shed, and the small bullseye was correspondingly bent and made even tinier. But, even here, the incomparable archer had hit it dead centre, and his arrow was held in place by a splinter it had dislodged.

Arjuna took the Gandiva off his back and strung it. He took an arrow from his quiver and sighted it carefully before letting it loose.

He missed. But it was such a narrow miss that the wind from its passing knocked the other arrow down.

Arjuna knew he had to meet this extraordinary marksman.

He came back the next evening, when the villagers had returned from the fields, and made inquiries.

The villagers gladly pointed out the bowman.

He turned out to be a young lad, barely out of his teens and quite scrawny.

'How do you shoot so accurately?' Arjuna asked him. 'Many years have I practiced, but I cannot match your performance.'

'It's easy,' said the boy, and willingly shared his secret. He shot the arrow first and then drew the target around it.

And right there is a lesson for us. We strive hard to reach a goal and frequently fail. Our arrow does not hit the target. We are then forlorn and disconsolate. But we can just as easily take whatever has transpired and embrace it fully. We can draw the bullseye around where the arrow has lodged itself. We may or may not be lauded as great archers, but our experience of life will become immeasurably better.

22

WHEN YOU FEEL REALLY TERRIBLE

I was miserable one weekend. I had caught some bug that was floating around and was running a fever of 103 degrees on Saturday. My wife was away, visiting my daughter, so I was alone in the house. The weather guy said it would warm up.

He lied.

Saturday was cold and rainy. Sunday was cold and not rainy—just grey.

Instead of feeling sorry for myself, I watched myself feeling sorry for myself.

I was congested and coughed frequently, bringing up thick phlegm every time. I began to feel sorry for myself and was about to wallow in self-pity.

And then I remembered my favourite quote from the Buddha. He told us that the mind determines your well-being. With this philosophy in mind, I thought I would experiment.

Instead of feeling sorry for myself, I watched myself feeling sorry for myself. It was as if I were a movie camera suspended a foot above my head, recording a close-up of all that was happening.

The self-pity vanished like dew in the tropical sun. In fact, it was so incongruous that I literally burst out laughing. I could watch my body labouring and heaving, and I had empathy but I was fine. No bemoaning, no complaints, just an acceptance that this is what is and that 'this, too, shall pass'.

Now, I was simply battling the flu and was not in great physical pain or in danger of leaving this mortal coil. But I wondered if the same detachment could hold under those circumstances.

The masters say it can, and their surety reinforced my intention to practise this some more. I hope that I don't have to test it under those circumstances any time soon.

But I will prepare to the best of my ability.

23

COPING WITH DISASTER

There are times, many times, when we feel overwhelmed. When everything that can go wrong, does. And when the universe, in a burst of creative energy, lays banana peels on our paths.

Don't despair!

You can cope using the technique I am about to share with you. It's simple. The solution can be used in an 'emergency situation', takes less than 5 minutes of your time and is very effective! Consider the case of poor Peter.

Peter was weary when he came to work. His three-year-old daughter, Alice, had been crying all night. She had an ear infection and would sleep for a few minutes at a time and then, energized, bawl for an hour. This went on for the entire night. His wife had an important presentation to make the following day and had departed to the guest bedroom, leaving him to cope.

He could not leave Alice at the preschool programme she normally went to, so he put in a desperate call to his mother who lived an hour away. She agreed to look after Alice but also managed to get in some pointed comments about how he was never available to talk anymore, and ended the conversation by asking why his wife was not doing a better job with Alice.

The traffic was horrendous, and he was late for his staff meeting. Just last week, he had made an issue about colleagues being late and suggested tartly that a little planning would help them arrive on time. Being late was discourteous to all, he had emphasized.

His admin handed him a note as he walked in. An important customer had just cancelled a large order. This meant that he was now behind his numbers for the quarter, instead of being comfortably ahead. And he had just sent out a memo to the analysts stating that sales were well over projection. How would this affect the coming IPO? He wasn't sure, but he knew that it would not help.

The phone rang. It was his wife. He had forgotten to cancel the appointment with the furnace service. A technician had tried the door and somehow set off the alarm and there were cops and firemen at the house. She asked him if he could please go there right away and set things straight? And he'd better do it fast, before they stepped on the flowering plants in the new patch around the door.

He wanted to shut his office door and howl. Emitting a primal scream seemed like an excellent idea.

What do you do when you have a day like this? We all have such days—or such moments in otherwise normal days.

First, sit upright with both feet on the ground and your spine straight.

Observe your breath going in, going out. Going in, going out. Going in, going out.

Second, breathe deeply and slowly. Most of the time we use the top third of our thoracic cavities while breathing. Change this. Continue breathing until you feel your stomach expanding gently and then feel it collapse as you exhale gently.

Observe your breath going in, going out. Going in, going out. Going in, going out. Do this for 2–3 minutes.

Your thoughts are running amuck, and your mental chatter is out of control. Worry is colliding with frustration as rage tries to take centre stage, only to be pushed aside by anxiety and fear. *Observe* all this happening.

Don't react from your emotions. *Pause* and continue breathing deeply.

The angry comment you were about to make. The blistering email you were ready to send. Ask yourself if they would really serve your long-term interests.

Then, from the morass of stuff clamouring for your attention, pick the one that is most important. Deal with it calmly. Quite possibly others are being frantic, but you will remain calm and let this rub off on them. This is how *you* develop presence. Not by appearing unruffled, but by actually *being* unruffled.

Then pick the next most important item and deal with it, again calmly. Keep going and keep breathing deeply, slowly.

Remember, no matter how 'bad' the day is, it will pass, and one day you will smile as you tell your grandson about the storms you had to weather.

The *pause* is a powerful tool and something you can use every day—even many times a day.

24

THE REAL REASON YOU GET ANGRY AND FEARFUL

Recently, I have fielded many calls from people in the grip of strong emotions, primarily anger and fear.

Do you become angry and/or afraid? Have you ever wondered why, in terms of whatever triggered these emotions in you? Most of us don't. Let's consider Steve.

Steve had a rough day at work.

His boss asked him to redo a report even though Steve had scrupulously adhered to the guidelines he had been given. The boss had changed his mind about what he needed. Instead of acknowledging this and apologizing, he blamed Steve for not giving him what he now wanted.

The HR clerk called to let Steve know that his expenses would not be reimbursed. True, he had stayed at a more expensive hotel than the guidelines permitted, but he had assumed that he could cover the extra charges with personal funds.

Not so. The clerk said there would be no reimbursement. He could probably get this reversed by going up the HR chain, but it would take up time he did not have and use up relationship capital he wanted to conserve.

As Steve entered his house that evening, he felt something under his foot and heard an ominous crack. He had just stepped on his son's brand-new Game Boy console. Steve had spoken to him many times about how it was inadvisable to leave stuff lying around.

Something inside him snapped. He took the stairs two at a time with flames shooting from his eyes. He was going to have a word with his son.

Why did Steve get angry? Why do you get angry? Steve thought that he got angry because his boss was inconsiderate, senseless rules ate up his time and his son was sloppy and careless.

All true, but these are surface explanations. Steve got angry because there was anger in him. You get angry because there is anger in you.

There is an Indian dessert called *rosogolla*. It is about the size of a ping-pong ball and white and very sweet. If you drop a *rosogolla* on the ground and step on it, what comes out is sugary syrup. You can beat it with a hammer, drop a suitcase on it or throw it against a wall. No matter how you mistreat and 'torture' it, all that comes out is sugary syrup.

Why? Because that's what's in the *rosogolla*.

In exactly the same way, anger flows out from you because it is inside you waiting for a time to erupt. Ditto for fear. And ditto for a whole host of other nasty denizens like jealousy and insecurity.

Anger flows out from you because it is inside you waiting for a time to erupt.

Life is wonderful. Think of life as a

skillful teacher that presents you with manifold triggers for each of these emotions to emerge. But they can only emerge because they are inside you. Recognize this. Don't beat yourself up about it. That will simply add to the anger you are already carrying.

Just begin the process of transmuting it. Here is a simple way of doing so. Earlier we talked about gratitude—an especially useful tool when it comes to dispelling negative emotions. Think about something in your life that is a true blessing, something you are grateful for.

It could be the peace you find when reading spiritual books. Or that you have a partner who genuinely cares for you. Or maybe it's the smile on your infant son's face when you look at him in his crib.

Whatever it is, savour it and let that feeling of gratitude well up from within you, and let it pour out of you in waves.

If you are a Type-A person, one who lives in your head—as most readers of this book are—it may take a while to go from 'thinking' gratitude to actually experiencing gratitude. Persist until this happens.

You will discover that it is impossible to be both grateful and angry at the same time. Try it. It does not work.

When your default emotional domain becomes that of gratitude, you will be like the *rosogolla* I spoke about. No matter what happens in your life, you will respond with care, compassion and reasoned action.

Not with anger.

And you will find that your life has been transformed for the better—infinitely for the better.

I have collected dozens of tips on how to effect such a transformation in your life, and I describe them in my book *Happiness at Work.*

25

DELIBERATE INTENT AND THE JOURNEYS YOU TAKE

I had a good day. I got a lot done, and many of the tasks I completed gave me a feeling of accomplishment. A client I had been coaching shared that after she began working with me she stopped feeling anxious, and was much happier. Others also noticed the change in her, and her husband asked her what was causing her unusual ebullience.

After dinner, my wife suggested watching a thriller. I assented readily. I like thrillers.

This one was dark. It had lots of gore in it. The violence was all too realistic, and unsavoury characters dished out a lot of it. After 40 minutes, my wife decided she had had enough and left. Sucked in, I finished the movie. And then regretted it.

It did not leave me with a pleasant feeling. It was neither pleasurable nor profitable.

I advise all my clients to move and behave with deliberate intent, and here I was acting with flagrant disregard for that excellent principle.

Think of your life as one long journey. You are born, and one day you will die. In between, there are lots of smaller journeys that you take, and each is a diversion.

When you read a book, watch a movie, hang out at a bar or play tennis, you go on a journey.

Just ask yourself, 'Is this a journey I want to take? Does it take me to a place where I want to spend time?'

If you sincerely ask yourself that question—and repeatedly ask it—your life will change.

Everything will alter—the kinds of movies you watch, the books you read, the friends you hang out with, the topics of conversation you bring up with the friends you hang out with, the leisure-time activities you indulge in, as well as a multitude of other aspects of your life.

The kind of thriller I watched? It took me to a place of gratuitous brutality and base emotions. A world where the way to combat violence is with greater violence.

No, it was not a place I wished to inhabit. Not even for a few minutes. But I spent a couple of hours there because of inertia.

That is where deliberate intent comes in.

Consciously and deliberately decide what emotional domain you would like to occupy. Then, examine the tools at your disposal that will help you get to that space and select an appropriate one.

Consciously and deliberately decide what emotional domain you would like to occupy.

On the night that I watched the movie, I was in possession of an excellent book on the life and teachings of a sage I greatly revere. His insights have had a profound impact on my understanding of life. I had the book at hand, and I would have loved reading it.

But I watched a crappy thriller instead. I was hijacked.

The way it happens is simple—a guy with a gun comes up to you when you are stopped at a traffic light, motions to you to unlock the car, slides into the passenger seat and makes you drive to a deserted locale miles away, and then…

I leave the rest to your imagination.

I venture to say that this is not an experience you would enjoy—certainly not one you would want to happen to you.

But, minus the guy with the gun, something like this happens to you all the time.

You come home from a hard day's work and turn on the idiot box. Netflix has a new series that you learnt about from an email with a tantalizing subject line that indicated it was just for you.

Fifteen minutes in and you realize that the best part of the thriller was the ad that promoted it. Inertia makes you finish the episode, and you wish you hadn't.

There are a ton of things you could have done that would have paid better dividends. You could have meditated. Finished that book you were deeply into. Organized your notes for the big meeting. Called your parents. Chatted with a good friend with whom you have lost touch.

But you watched that lousy Netflix show, and you didn't even enjoy it.

You were hijacked.

Cognoscenti talk about the 'attention economy'. This is simply a fancy way of saying that everybody wants you to notice what they would like you to notice.

Politicians make outrageous statements and are openly combative. The more they rant, the more people pay attention to them. Some cheer and egg them on. Some get affronted.

But everyone notices them.

They are the 'winners' in the attention economy.

You are the loser. You let your emotional domain be hijacked by someone else's agenda. You were sad or angry or appalled or horrified or infuriated because that was what someone wanted you to be.

It is also possible to be enlightened, inspired or uplifted, but this is rare.

Strong negative emotions create a vortex into which you are easily sucked. That is why newscasts always feature some tragedy in some part of the world. The anchor gravely describes the horror. He—or she—may seem to be saying 'tut-tut' but is actually promoting this anxiety.

It is not common to hear about something that is going well, something that lifts your spirits.

Check this out for yourself. Watch one week of your favourite news programme and tabulate the number of stories that leave you feeling morose about the state of the world, versus the number that leave you feeling energized and full of hope.

I rest my case.

This sad situation has been so for decades. What is new today is the number of ways in which you can be assaulted.

That is the contribution of social media.

There is a simple way out of this morass. You can struggle out of the quicksand. The tool to use is deliberate intent, and it means that you choose the emotional domain that you occupy. If you do not do this, others will happily choose for you. They have been doing it all along and will continue.

So, if the domain you decide to occupy is one of tranquil contemplation, you will pay no attention to Netflix blandishments and you will not watch that junk series. So, in advance, consciously, mindfully, decide which journeys you will take. And when you will take them.

You will still be derailed at times, and also hijacked. But this will happen less frequently.

And you will find that your experience of life improves. Dramatically!

26

IS HE REALLY SUCH A JERK?

Are there people in your life who inflame you and leave you a quivering jelly of frustration and indignation?

You can develop ulcers. Or you can reframe the situation. Here is a story that illustrates it beautifully.

The school was in a depressed neighbourhood and had many at-risk children. Jason earned relatively good grades and had a pretty decent track record as far as behaviour went, but of late he seemed to be slipping into the same spiral of shifty rootlessness that affected so many of the adolescent youths in his class.

Julie was a dedicated teacher, genuinely desiring to make a difference in the lives of her students. But she found it harder and harder to keep her enthusiasm up. Many of the kids were physically large and imposing. Last week, one of them had hit her when she remonstrated with him. He would have continued his assault if his classmates had not restrained him. She had never felt fear before, but now it followed her around relentlessly. She wondered if this was how veterans returning from war-torn countries felt.

Jason had his head down when she entered her class. He did not look up. He had been dozing a lot of late, and she took it as another sign of him flouting her authority. She asked him a question. He did not reply. A soft snore emanated from him as if he were deliberately provoking her.

Whether deliberate or not, it worked. She walked up to him and asked him the same question in a louder, confrontational manner. He jerked his head up, and there was fury in his eyes. 'Leave me alone,' he snarled.

She fled from the classroom and went straight to the principal's office. Two burly security officers escorted Jason off the school premises.

She pressed for indefinite suspension. She was afraid of facing Jason again. Her face still hurt from the blow she had received the previous week.

One of the older teachers asked Julie and the principal to hold off on any further action for twenty-four hours while he investigated the matter.

He met with the principal and Julie the next day.

It turned out that Jason's father was in jail and had been for years. His mother was struggling to keep Jason and his sister in school while fighting her own addiction, and dealing with the domestic abuse of her boyfriend. Jason had been caring for his sister and his mother while also trying to keep up with his schoolwork.

The previous night had been trying. A fever had kept his sister up all night. Jason tended to her and to his mother, who was comatose from a drinking binge. Then he came to school and fell asleep from sheer tiredness. He snapped when woken. He desperately needed rest and

> could not control himself.
>
> 'We should give him a medal,' said the older teacher, 'but we were about to throw him out and further wreck his life.'
>
> The senior teacher and Julie met with Jason together. Julie shared what it felt like to be knocked down by a student and the fear it engendered. Jason spoke about the helplessness he felt as all the adults in his life—who should have been role models—became parasites, sucking energy out of him.
>
> A bond developed between Julie and Jason. She became his advocate, was able to find rehab resources for his mother, and counselled him through difficult times until he graduated.

Julie and Jason came perilously close to a conflict in which they would both have lost. There is a lesson in why it almost happened. Each of them viewed the other through the prism of their own experience, and neither recognized that this is what they were doing.

Each of them viewed the other through the prism of their own experience, and neither recognized that this is what they were doing.

Are you confronting behaviour that enrages you? Think about plausible scenarios where this behaviour could actually be reasonable.

Don't get hung up on whether the scenario you construct is 'true'. It does not matter in the slightest whether or not it is. The very act of visualizing such possibilities opens you up.

You recognize that your take of the situation is not the only one, and this takes you to a different emotional domain.

And because you are open to the possibility that the other person could have a valid reason for his or her behaviour, your interaction is markedly improved. And the results are pleasantly surprising.

Does this work every single time? Of course not. But it works often enough that your life becomes significantly better.

27

THE TELEMARKETER AND ME

If I were to make a list of the top five things that bring me joy, 'listening to a telemarketer make his pitch' would not make that list. Between you and me, it would not make the list of 2,000 things that bring me joy either. When the National Do Not Call Registry was announced a few years ago, I signed up immediately.

The do-not-call list does not work. Those pesky creatures get through anyway.

What *really* annoys me is that telemarketers have also started calling me on my cell phone. Yet, I learned a valuable lesson from a telemarketer. You might be missing out on a similar opportunity.

> I was talking to my daughter recently, right before I was due to drive her to the airport. We were having a lively discussion on a topic that escapes me.
>
> My cell phone rang.
>
> I did not recognize the number, but I had recently posted a blog that was well received so I took the call, in case it was a fan. A somewhat nasal voice mispronounced my name and wanted to know how my day was going.

'Who are you and why are you calling?' I responded. I was loud and not very polite. He tried to explain who he was, and I got rid of him by hanging up.

My daughter's jaw dropped. 'You were so rude to him, Daddy,' she expostulated. 'I've never heard you shout like that before!'

'He does it all the time,' my wife interjected helpfully.

I tried to explain that, on the scale of evolution, telemarketers were somewhere between primordial slime and amoebae but my daughter was having none of it.

'He was only trying to do his job and he probably hates it, and you just made it even more awful for him,' she said.

I told her that I had no interest in buying anything.

'You don't have to buy what he is trying to sell,' she replied. 'But you could have been nicer to him. You had the opportunity to make the world a little nicer for a fellow human being, and you totally blew it.'

And then she delivered the coup de grâce.

'Isn't that what you teach in your course?'

I threw in the towel. Yes, I was being totally me-centered. Yes, I had given no thought whatsoever to the feelings of said telemarketer and countless others before him. At the back of my mind lurked the feeling that, if enough persons were like me all telemarketers would quit and the profession would become deservedly extinct, but I did not express it.

My daughter changed my train of thought—and exposed a blind spot in which you could have parked a tractor-trailer.

How many persons do we run across whom we cavalierly ignore? Janitors? Waitresses? Cab drivers? Bellhops? Lawn-care workers? Each is a human being with their own cares and dreams. Each provides a valuable service that we need, but many of us barely acknowledge it. And we don't even recognize that we are being callous. We are so self-absorbed in our busyness that we totally miss the opportunity to enhance someone else's life, and hence our own.

How many persons do we run across whom we cavalierly ignore? Janitors? Waitresses? Cab drivers? Bellhops? Lawn-care workers?

Guiltily, I recalled that my wife put out ice-cold bottles of water for our lawn-care workers and the mailman on really hot days. I applauded the sentiment but did not even think of doing something similar when the mercury soared and she was away.

I will endeavour to change. I may not buy candy for the next telemarketer who reaches me, but I will be conscientious and not bite his head off.

And, for a brief instant, I will acknowledge that fate has intertwined us for some unfathomable purpose and will seek to make his life a little better through genuine interaction.

The world may be a better place if we all do likewise.

28

WHAT TO DO ABOUT THE *BEEP*!

Alan Gassman, a prominent Florida attorney, took my capstone programme, Creativity and Personal Mastery, a few years ago. Shortly thereafter, he invited me to Tampa to meet some of his clients. He gave me a bunch of books that had an impact on him, and among them was an inconspicuous paperback with a light-blue cover. It was called *The Untethered Soul: The Journey Beyond Yourself* and was by someone called Michael Alan Singer.

I gave many talks during that visit, and an affable gentleman who had asked some excellent questions came up to me after one of them and asked me if I had read the aforementioned book. I assured him that I had not, and he strongly recommended it.

I came back to New York and discovered that I had two copies of *The Untethered Soul* on my bookshelves. I buy lots of books, and my wife is convinced that Amazon's share price run-up is entirely due to my activity. Somehow, somewhere, something had made enough of an impression on me that I had ordered the book. Twice.

I now had three copies of Singer's book.

I can recognize when the universe is nudging me.

I read the book. It instantly made it to the 'life-changing

books' section of my syllabus. I have since recommended it to many. Andre Vögtlin, an executive recruiter based in Basel and a prominent executive with the Swiss Chess Federation, who is also an alumnus of my programme, called the book 'spiritual TNT'.

I concur.

The Untethered Soul is not a book to read and set aside. You must let the ideas in it seep into your mind and take root there. When you do this, and what you have planted has grown from a sapling to a mighty tree, you find yourself living in an indescribably better world.

A little while later, I got on a plane to Gainesville, Florida. I just had to meet Michael Singer. Mickey, as he prefers to be called, had graciously agreed to a private meeting at his yoga and meditation centre, Temple of the Universe. Afterward, he took me in his car to show me around the temple property. We talked about many things, and he acquiesced to remaining in touch.

He has a way of starkly showing us the ridiculous predicaments we are all stuck in, and the ridiculously easy way to get ourselves unstuck.

The paradox is that it is both supremely easy and exceptionally difficult at the same time. Here is one of the game changers he threw out in his talk at the temple, on the Sunday I visited.

> You are driving and stop at a red light when your smartphone vibrates. You take a quick glance at it, and your brain registers that it is a message to which you have to respond. Even as you do this, there is a *beep* from the car behind you. The light has changed.

You shake your head and move on. *Geez*, you think. *What's with that guy? Where the hell does he think he's going and who the hell does he think he is? People are so impatient these days.*

When he pulls up beside you at the next light, you glare at him. He studiously avoids looking at you.

That *beep* bothered you. It was just a trivial *beep*, but it threw you off your stride. It coloured your day and made it a little worse. If you let such a minor disruption upset you, what will happen when you have to deal with your uncompromising ex-husband or your contentious son or your irritated boss?

No wonder we are all stressed out and desperately seeking to meditate or be mindful or practice yoga as a means of holding it all together.

There is an astonishingly simple way out. There is a moment when you hear the *beep* that you can decide, 'Am I going to let this disturb me?'

You can decide that you will not let it disturb you. You can be the observer that hears the *beep*, and as this observer you can decide to let it go.

You can also decide not to let your irritated boss or your contentious son or your uncompromising ex-husband disturb you.

This does not mean that you don't do what you must. It means that you do it from the knowledge that you are doing what you can in the best way possible, and you are at peace with the outcome whatever it may be. It does not disturb your equanimity because you have decided that it will not.

It really is that simple.

It is ridiculously easy.

It is unbelievably hard.

I am going to speak about an important step you can take to let go of the inner disturbance that life produces so, so often. Wanting to let it go is not the same thing as being able to do so. Here's how you can choose inner peace even when you feel like you have stumbled into a tornado. It is a powerful strategy that can help you greatly.

Step 1: Examine your life as it is right now and make a list of all the things that disturb you, with some predictability. For example, you may be bothered by your daughter refusing to take college seriously and hanging out with a boyfriend you think is unsuitable; you feel your career has stalled and you are stuck in a dead-end job with no way out; or you have concerns about your relationship with your spouse and wonder if you should stay in your marriage.

> *When you have consciously and explicitly recognized that this could happen and what you will do if it does, it loses its power to terrify you.*

Step 2: In each case, think of the worst-case scenario. Your daughter may drop out of college and run off with her unsuitable paramour, who leaves her when she becomes pregnant. You may get fired with no notice, and your spouse may leave you before you decide whether you wish to remain married.

Step 3: Recognize that this worst-case scenario is just a thought in your head. It may come to pass or it may not happen. In any event, imagine that it transpires and come up with what you will do if and when it happens.

Here is the secret: When you have consciously and explicitly recognized that this could happen and what you will do if it does, it loses its power to terrify you. Make your peace with that worst case scenario. You hope it won't happen. But if it does, you now know what you intend to do.

Step 4: Go about your business, and take steps that will prevent the undesirable scenario from coming about. Focus relentlessly on your intent and what you are doing. Don't even think about what could happen. You have no control over the outcome, so why waste your energy worrying?

If you pour your energy into what you are doing, you will feel peace rather than turbulence.

Repeat these steps for every situation that disturbs you. It is a simple process and, once you get the hang of it, you will find that it works in a vast range of situations.

Begin implementing this tactic in your life right away and see what a difference it makes.

29

WHAT WILL THEY THINK OF ME?

Let me talk allegorically, just to keep it interesting.

You think everyone is watching a particular movie. But they are not.

You are the only one watching this movie with attention.

But you don't know this.

And this harms you in many ways and prevents you from living the full life you are capable of.

I will explain.

As a professor and an elite coach, I frequently run into individuals who do not attempt things they feel inclined to because they feel embarrassed. They are overly concerned about 'What will they think of me?'

> Carmen was a good manager and well-liked by both her bosses and the executives who reported to her.
>
> Her team was elected to stage a skit at the annual Company Day festivities.
>
> It was uproariously funny, and they wanted her to be part of it. Her character would be scruffy and suffer a fall and then recover to brilliantly crush the department bully with a verbal riposte.

Her boss and his boss would be there, watching the skit and they had never seen her when she was not polished and professionally dressed.

She was concerned about her image and declined to participate.

Has something like this ever happened to you? Have you turned down an unusual assignment or a lateral move that you would have liked to take but for the fear of 'What will they think of me?' Have you declined a public-speaking opportunity or an invitation to join an improvisation group, or hesitated to speak up at a meeting where there was an expert in the room for the same reason?

We all want others to think well of us. And we all want to know what 'they' think of us. Well, I have good news for you. I know exactly what they think of you. And I will tell you right now.

We all want others to think well of us. And we all want to know what 'they' think of us.

The truth is they don't think of you at all. And they won't suddenly start doing so either.

You go through life watching the movie of your life, and you think everyone is watching it as well. But they are not. They are busy watching the movie of *their* life.

And in that movie, you have only a small part—if indeed you have any part at all.

Don't take my word for it. Here is how you can check it out for yourself. Hundreds of my students have come to ruefully tell me that I was right.

Go back a few years and recollect some situation—business or personal—where you made a horrible gaffe. You did something so gauche that your face burned, and you wished you could sink into the floor or take an extended trip to Abyssinia.

Possibly your ears are still burning as you recall the incident.

Now, visit or call up the persons who were present there at the time. Do it today and gently broach the subject and ask for their recollection.

I will wager that most will not recall the event, and those who do will think it of no significance. And you have spent years being bothered by your emotions and your faulty recollections. Your fear of being negatively appraised by others is keeping you from trying out stuff that your heart calls you to.

It is affecting your career choices and, potentially, making you decide to stay in a job you hate rather than break off to start your own company. It is preventing you from trying to get to know that person you find really attractive.

Recognize that 'What will they think of me?' is a prison. It is a prison that you have constructed, and it does not really exist—because *they* are not thinking of you at all. Break out of this invisible but ever-so-strong prison. Do it today!

30

OUR MISERY IS CAUSED BY RESISTANCE

All of our misery, all of our pain, is caused by our resistance to the way life is unfolding. Fortunately, there is a remedy. Joy comes from total acceptance of what is.

As you go through life, observe how you are continuously wedded to your preferences. If you are like most, you want the world to unfurl in a manner that pleases you.

This may come as a shock to you because you think of yourself as 'easy-going' and 'open-minded'. Nevertheless, you are a control freak. You just don't admit it or recognize it in yourself.

This control freakishness manifests itself in subtle ways. Flashes of irritation when things don't go your way, such as when a dithering driver can't make up his mind which way to go. When he finally does turn, his delay causes you to get stopped by the long red light at a busy intersection.

Or the thrill you feel when the player you are rooting for wins Wimbledon, or the team you are cheering becomes the Superbowl champion.

You want people to laugh uproariously at your jokes, applaud your speech and recognize you for the kind, wonderful and generous being you are. And in ways, big and small, you alter your behaviour in a manner that you think will get you the response you want.

Yes, you are a control freak. You just don't admit it, and you point to someone who is even more so as proof that you are not.

You want people to laugh uproariously at your jokes, applaud your speech and recognize you for the kind, wonderful and generous being you are.

Here is a radical idea for you.

Can you try to accept what comes without trying to make things happen the way you would like them to?

Can you want what comes rather than trying manifest what you want? Can you train your desires? Actually, you can and the following story serves to demonstrate this principle. Swami Dayananda was a teacher of Vedanta who always got gales of laughter when he told this tale.

Devout Indian women consider it a great honour if a sage comes to their house for a meal. They are not above indulging in one-upmanship such as, 'The swami only came to your house for breakfast, but he came to my house for dinner.'

Swami Dayananda was visiting a new city for a 10-day Vedanta camp and lunching at the home of a devotee. She had prepared an elaborate feast and loaded his plate with many items. One of these was a curry made from *karela*—bitter gourd—that he did not like at all.

He decided to finish it first so he could then relish the items he liked. It is bad form to waste food, so he swallowed the karela curry and washed it down with water.

His hawk-eyed hostess noted this and, before he could protest, ladled a double serving of karela curry on his plate. Swami Dayananda, with great difficulty, finished eating all of it.

There is an effective grape vine used by devotee housewives. The next housewife to host Swami Dayananda asked the previous one what dishes he preferred and was told that he really liked karela curry because he finished it first, and then enjoyed the second portion she gave him.

And wherever Swami Dayananda went, hospitable wives and mothers prepared large quantities of karela curry for him.

At this point in the story, Swami Dayananda would pause for impact and deliver the punch line.

'So, I decided to like karela curry and it is now one of my favourite dishes!'

It is an amusing tale and, when delivered by a master raconteur, leaves the audience in stitches. But there is also a lesson in it.

What would you have done? Would you have got the word out that you really did not like karela curry? Would you even have hinted at or outright stated your culinary desires?

Would you have tried to impose your preferences on the world, or would you have let it unfold as Swami Dayananda did?

As you go through life, consciously recognize how much you are bound and ruled by your preferences, your likes and dislikes.

And gently, ever so gently, let some of them go.

When that dithering driver causes you to be stuck at the red light, smile and wish him well. Beam out goodwill.

Try this for a week and see how it changes your experience of life.

31

HOW TO HAVE A TERRIFIC DAY, EVERY DAY

Would you like to have a fantastic day, every day?

Of course you would.

But already the sceptical wheels are turning in your head because you know this is 'impossible'. And you will read on because while you know that every day cannot possibly be fantastic, maybe you will learn something that will make some days fantastic.

But I am serious. Every day can be a blast if you let go of a foolish belief that you have. Just discard the false notion you carry that you can't enjoy each and every day, and each day will become richly rewarding!

Just discard the false notion you carry that you can't enjoy each and every day, and each day will become richly rewarding!

Let me explain.

I meet lots of people and talk to many more over the phone or Skype or Zoom. I ask them how they are and get responses like 'hanging in there', 'can't complain', 'well, thank you' and 'okay'.

A rare few say 'super' or 'fantastic'. More say 'terrible' or 'could be better'.

I will show you how you can have a terrific day, every day. It is simple, and you will understand how simple it is when I explain it. It can also be ridiculously easy or fiendishly difficult, depending on how open you are to accepting new ideas and implementing them in your life.

Here is what you must do to have a superlative day today and every day: When you wake up in the morning, make a conscious, mindful decision that you are going to have a fantastic day.

Don't laugh.

This really works.

The problem that most people have is that they confuse having a terrific day with two things that have nothing to do with it.

But they never examine their beliefs about these two things and get stuck in erroneous thinking, and then have terrible days as a result.

What is this erroneous thinking? I bet you are also guilty of this. You believe that for you to have a terrific day, (i) stuff that you want should happen, and (ii) stuff that you do not want should not happen.

So, you are all set to have a great day and then your car does not start. When you finally get on the road, somebody sideswipes you, leaving a long scratch and a dent on your car. He doesn't stop, so you don't get his licence plate number. You are late for your meeting, the deal you were hoping to close has to be postponed and your prospect's secretary does not book another appointment for you because she says he is 'thinking it over'.

So, it is turning out to be a lousy day, right?

Only if you let it become lousy.

Lots of stuff happened. You would rather it did not happen.

But it did. Why compound the problem by releasing your intention of having a terrific day?

Think about it. Feces will drop from the sky. It always does. That is the nature of life.

When feces drop from the sky, you have to put aside your plans and do some clean-up work. But that does *not* mean you cannot have a terrific day. It simply means that there is some unexpected clean-up that you need to put into your terrific day.

When unexpected, unwanted stuff happens, simply ask it, as if it were a person, 'Am I going to let you steal my fantastic day from me?'

If you can truly get into the habit of doing this, you will be surprised at how many of your days become marvellous. And no, this is not a well-meaning but impossible-to-heed pablum, unless you decide it is.

So, give it a try!

32

BE GRATEFUL THAT YOU ARE NOT SPECIAL

I am going to say something that flies in the face of accepted wisdom. Dozens, hundreds, thousands of gurus tell you the opposite of what I am about to share with you. There are courses that enjoin you to believe something that is flat-out wrong, and yet this falsehood is lauded as the way out of the problems that beset you.

Your indoctrination begins at a very young age—before grade school, even in pre-kindergarten. In early years, it does little damage and can even be beneficial. In later years, it becomes toxic and corrosive.

I have a confession to make. This falsehood is so firmly entrenched in our culture that I have sometimes used it myself to get a point across or to accomplish some end.

The big lie is this: You are told right from childhood that you are special. That you are unique. That you are significant. That you *matter*.

When you are very young, you don't quite understand what this means. All you know is that the adults who mouth this look at you lovingly, cuddle you and give you treats.

This is good. It feels good and helps you grow.

However, as you grow older, the toxic side effects of this indulgence appear.

You see that you are not particularly special. But you like the *feeling* of being special. So, you try to recreate it by *trying* to become significant in some restricted playing field.

Do you like tennis? You know you will not win a Grand Slam tournament, but perhaps you can win the club championship. Or be the top player in your league at the club.

We are *always* striving. To accomplish something. To become something. To acquire something.

I frequently ask those who take my programmes to become the best version of themselves that they are capable of being. And I will continue to do this. It has value for many and fits into the cultural conditioning we have all been subject to.

But, on a different plane, this striving is pointless.

A rose blooms. It does not go all out to become the best rose it can be. Its beauty is effortless. It does not feel diminished because there is a 'better' rose next to it; nor does it feel superior to the rose beside it that bloomed earlier and is now fading. Its innocent naturalness is why we admire it.

A rose blooms. It does not go all out to become the best rose it can be. Its beauty is effortless.

Your accomplishments, your possessions, your fame, your paltry triumphs are all in time and space. And whatever is in time and space will be wrested from you and scattered to the winds.

It used to be said, 'The sun never set on the British Empire.' Where is it now? The Mughal Empire comprised more than a quarter of the world's economy in its day. Gone!

James Shirley, in his poem 'The Glories of Our Blood and State' says it beautifully:

> The glories of our blood and state
> Are shadows, not substantial things;
> There is no armour against Fate;
> Death lays his icy hand on kings:
> Sceptre and Crown
> Must tumble down,
> And in the dust be equal made
> With the poor crooked scythe and spade.

But we *need* to feel special. To feel superior. When Copernicus and Galileo postulated that perhaps the Earth revolved around the Sun and not the other way around, the 'specialness' of the Earth was diminished and both men suffered in the ensuing uproar.

So let me repeat it again: You are *not* special. There have been millions like you in the past and there will be millions more in years to come. Even if you are Caesar or Genghis Khan or Alexander, you will shrivel and die and be forgotten.

That is the way of life.

And it is beautiful.

Do you *matter*?

Yes, you do, but in the same way that an individual bee in a hive matter or a grain of sand on a beach.

The world will get along just fine if you were to disappear today. If you can relax into this knowledge, it is liberating. You no longer have to put up and maintain a façade. You can be who you are—a free spirit that cannot be bound in a cage of flesh or hemmed in by desire.

When you are not driven by restless ambition, you can

flower where you are and experience the 'peace that passeth all understanding'.*

So, where does that leave you? Should you cease to set goals, benchmark your progress or try to get promoted or make more money?

Of course not. You *can't* stop any of this, even if you had an intellectual interest in doing so.

You do all of this, but you do it the same way a rose blooms. You do it not because you *want* anything but because this activity is part of the natural unfolding of life for you.

This is a profound insight, and I have done it scant justice in my brief explanation. Putting it in play in your life is a lifetime's work.

---

*Philippians 4:7

33

AMBITION IS BAD FOR YOU

I heard of Horatio Alger long before I came to the US. My father gave me a book titled *Lives of Poor Boys Who Became Famous*. One of my father's friends, who was present when he gifted it to me, commented that they were like real Horatio Alger stories.

Later, I read many Horatio Alger stories. One of them—*In a New World*—is still on my shelf.

The stories are mostly about teenage boys who, born into poverty, nevertheless made it to fame and fortune by dint of hard work, luck and driving ambition. I have heard many business leaders say that they look for ambitious youngsters, and many politicians cite lack of ambition as the reason the destitute remain so.

What about you?

Are you ambitious? Do you regard ambition as an admirable virtue? Do you wish you had more of it churning in your veins? Most importantly, do you wish you were like someone with tremendous ambition who reached some high position?

This is the fool's journey that our society sends us on. Ask yourself: Would you drink corrosive acid? Then why harbour ambition?

The dictionary definition of ambition is 'an earnest desire for some type of achievement or distinction, as power, honor, fame, or wealth and the willingness to strive for its attainment'.*

And there is the rub. When you are ambitious, you live for a future that may or may not come. And even if it does come, it will not be what you expected and it will never give you the joy, peace and well-being you hoped it would.

When you are ambitious, you live for a future that may or may not come.

In the days when Córdoba was a vibrant, cosmopolitan city with dozens of libraries and monuments, and London and Paris were mere overgrown hovels, the Caliph of Córdoba, Abd-al-Rahman III, ruminated thus:

> I have now reigned above fifty years in victory or peace; beloved by my subjects, dreaded by my enemies, and respected by my allies. Riches and honors, power and pleasure, have waited on my call, nor does any earthly blessing appear to have been wanting to my felicity. In this situation, I have diligently numbered the days of pure and genuine happiness which have fallen to my lot: they amount to Fourteen: —O man! place not thy confidence in this present world!**

I frequently get pushback when I advocate giving up ambition. People like to say, 'Why should I get up in the morning if I don't have ambition? How will anything change in the world—how will any improvement or advancement take place—if not

*'ambition', *Dictionary.com*, https://tinyurl.com/3jjx64n8. Accessed on 11 August 2023.

**Gibbon, Edward, *The History of the Decline and Fall of the Roman Empire*, Vol. 5, CreateSpace Independent Publishing Platform, 2015.

for ambitious persons who make things happen and will not rest until they achieve their goals?'

Before we can answer questions like this, we should spend a moment in reflection.

Ambition, by definition, makes you unhappy with your lot. It sows seeds of despair and the notion that 'tomorrow will be better if I get whatever my ambition leads me to desire'.

Pay heed to the words of Abd-al-Rahman.

Tomorrow will not be better. Neither will the day after. And this has nothing to do with the toys you acquire or the power you wrest. It is just the nature of desire and the way it is whipped into unrest by your monkey mind.

Gabriel looked out at the rolling lawns of his mansion. A bright sun was causing the air to shimmer over the flagstone walkways. There were flowers in profusion in their own carefully-tended beds—dahlias, chrysanthemums, roses, peonies and delphiniums. There were water lilies and lotuses in their own special pond. It was a sight to soothe the troubled breast.

But not Gabriel's breast. His heart was heavy.

It was his birthday, and his three children had all called to wish him a happy day. They had sent baskets of goodies he could not consume, items his doctor had warned him to stay away from. No one visited, and no one expressed regret at not being there.

Life was hectic. His children had their careers to build, and their kids had soccer and tennis and piano and karate and...God knows what else. Anyway, what was the point of visiting a crotchety old codger whose left side was paralysed and whose speech was barely intelligible.

It was not supposed to be like this. Coming from desperate poverty, Gabriel had struggled to make good. He did not belong to the right circles and was unable to get a position at any of the well-known financial institutions, so he joined a scrappy investment bank where he worked hard.

There were lots of immigrant physicians in New York. Many felt they were outsiders, and he connected with them. He got a bright idea. His surgeon friends treated accident victims and could give him details of their injuries and likelihood of recovery. He used this to calculate the probable damages the victims could collect from the insurance company or companies involved. He persuaded his bank to buy the litigation from the victims. They got a fraction of what the eventual settlement would have been, but many were happy to accept because it was immediate cash.

After a few such transactions, he broadened his vision. He set up a division of his company to buy hundreds of such litigations, package them into tranches and sell them as securities. He had a hunch that pension funds and institutional investors would be open to such investments in an era of low interest rates.

His instinct was correct. He succeeded. He became wealthy beyond his wildest dreams.

He also missed his kids' performances, family dinners and at least one graduation. Somewhere along the line, his wife walked out. There were no bitter fights, no acrimony. She just informed him she was leaving and left. The children were grown, and she did not ask for alimony or a share of his assets. His wealth was all his.

He bought his mansion with a vague notion that he would reconcile with his wife and somehow his children would come back, and they would all live happily together. But then he had a stroke—and a second one while being taken to the hospital. Now, he was permanently paralysed on his left side and not too facile on his right.

He could afford the best possible care, but the nurses, the therapists and the aides who worked on his shrivelled body could not still the shrill, insistent voice in his head. The voice that was becoming louder. The voice that told him he had wasted his life and destroyed himself in pursuit of his ambition.

A sad tale, and it reinforces the words of the Caliph of Córdoba.

That said, do create and maintain a grand vision and work toward it because that is your path in life and it feels right to walk along that path. Your activity will not be driven by ambition if you fully recognize that your reward does not lie in achieving whatever you set out to do. Your gain comes from the *effort* you put into attaining it. That effort is what produces the learning and the growth, and the change in you that is a true blessing.

It will be wonderful if you achieve your goal—no problem if you do not. On this road, you will always win.

Think about it.

One final note: You may agree with what I have just said, but you will not be able to give up ambition easily or as an act of volition.

Persist, however, and one day you will find that ambition is no longer the cat-o'-nine-tails driving you on.

34

A LESSON ON SERENITY AND HAPPINESS FROM *MY FAIR LADY*

One summer day, both my children were visiting us. We went to see *My Fair Lady*. It is my all-time favourite play and we had fabulous seats. Afterward, we went backstage and I told Lauren Ambrose what a superb job she did as Eliza Doolittle; and Ted Sperling how great the music was.

I also stargazed a little. Mandy Patinkin was right behind me. I tried to avoid staring, but he also came backstage and we bumped into each other five times. The twinkle in his eyes said we should stop meeting like this, so I told him—truthfully—that he was my favourite character in *Homeland*.

We had a lovely dinner after that. It was a magical day.

It also got me thinking.

A powerful moment in *My Fair Lady* is when Henry Higgins's mother commiserates with a sobbing Eliza Doolittle. Eliza is distraught because Higgins did not congratulate her after an exemplary performance at the royal ball, when the crown prince himself took the first dance with her.

She rebukes Higgins by comparing him to Colonel Pickering, who treats a flower girl as if she were a duchess. Higgins retorts that he treats a duchess as if she were a flower girl, and asserts that he treats everyone the same.

Eliza wanted to feel important and be treated that way.

So do you. So do I. And so does everyone else.

Every time our emotional well-being is affected by whether someone else acknowledges us, we construct a prison around ourselves and hand that person the key.

The problem arises when we want this recognition and applause to come from a specific person or group of persons. Every time our emotional well-being is affected by whether someone else acknowledges us, we construct a prison around ourselves and hand that person the key.

Why would we do that? Why would we *ever* want to do that?

We do it because we have never thought about it, and because everyone around us is doing the same. Do we really want our happiness to be controlled by the spigot of other people's attention and acclaim?

As I stated before, your job as a flower is to bloom. Your fulfilment lies in that.

The rose that blossoms in the wild is not a whit less than the one that does so in a show garden.

Think about this. Think about how you are constantly basking in the acclaim of others, and trying to obtain it and more of it.

You don't need it.

And the best way to free yourself is to see—*really see*—how this quest is robbing you of your birthright: serenity and happiness.

35

YES, YOU CAN REWRITE YOUR PAST!

I cannot even count the number of clients who have come to me, bemoaned their circumstances and then attributed their current situation to something that happened in their past. Some awful tragedy, some dire misfortune, some unfortunate event whose long arm is still clutching their throat.

Some have risen from their adversity and flourished. Some have sunk into despair. Some have hovered in between—partially free but still unable to release themselves from the nightmare of their past.

All are firm about one thing: There is nothing they can do about their past.

Do you feel the same way? Are you bound, chained and immobilized by what you thought happened to you?

You are dead wrong.

The events that happened in your life don't matter all that much. The stories you tell yourself about those events matter a great deal. Consider the tale of Joe and Frank, for instance.

> Joe watched through the window as Frank and his friends climbed into the limo. They were going to spend winter break at Frank's home. Estate, actually. Frank's father was

a successful financier, and his family lived well. Joe had not been invited. *He needs me to help him with his homework but doesn't want to have anything to do with me outside class or study hall*, thought Joe bitterly as the bile rose in his throat.

Neither of Joe's parents had gone to school. His mother was a domestic worker. His father did odd jobs when he could find them—hanging wallpaper, painting houses, chopping wood. Both parents fiercely valued education and were determined that their son would do better than they had. By chance, his father discovered that the summer home whose lawn he was mowing belonged to the headmaster of an elite private school. Mustering all his courage, he begged the headmaster to do something for his son.

The headmaster was a kind man and summoned Joe for an interview. Joe had raw intelligence and grim determination, and the educator felt an instinctive liking for him. He arranged for Joe to come to his school on a scholarship. And so, Joe left home for the first time and went to an upper-class boarding school. Hard work never bothered him, and he grabbed the opportunity with both hands. Within a year, he was at the top of his class—an academic superstar.

Social life was something else. The scholarship paid for tuition and room and board, but there was little left for frivolities or fun. Joe was also required to work in the school library, and this ate up his free time. He could not afford to go to the theatre in town or hang out in pubs and bars and clubs as his classmates did. They were underage, but they drank and had a good time. Joe felt excluded.

Frank was his idol. He was handsome, captain of the soccer team, opening batsman in cricket and a good fencer. The other kids turned away when they saw Joe's shabby clothes, winced when they heard his thick accent and ignored him. But Frank was always civil. Frank even asked Joe for help in math, and the two of them studied together and had long conversations.

Frank invited Joe out with a group of his friends. When they were at the bar, a talking head on the big-screen TV announced that a Princeton mathematician had solved Fermat's Last Theorem. Joe was so enthralled that the others asked him what was up. He gave a brief description of the centuries-old mathematical puzzle that had not been solved until then. It had stumped the best mathematicians in the world for three centuries. Joe was so earnest that the others started tittering and the conversation soon turned to girls and football.

Frank never invited him out again.

I should have known he was ashamed of me, thought Joe bitterly as he watched the limo exit the school gates.

A month later, Frank asked him if he would like to spend the weekend at his place. A thrill ran through Joe. He was mistaken! Frank was not ashamed of him after all!

'Who else will be there?' he asked excitedly.

'Why, no one,' said Frank hesitantly. 'It'll be just the two of us. My parents are away, so we'll have the place to ourselves.'

A hot burning rage of humiliation settled on Joe. He had been right all along. Frank did not want to be seen associating with him. The invitation was his consolation prize for helping Frank with math, physics and lab work.

Frank was putting up with him for the weekend. 'No thanks,' he said gruffly as he strode off. He was darned if he would accept such charity.

Years passed, but the hurt rankled. Joe became partner at a prestigious consulting firm. He got pulled into a meeting with the CEO of a company his firm was pitching. He walked in well prepared and ran into Frank. He was the outside attorney, and the CEO had specifically called him in to evaluate the deal and bless it if it passed muster.

A hot ball of lead formed inside Joe and settled in his stomach. He knew he no longer had any chance of landing the contract, and seriously contemplated walking out. Doing so would have been unprofessional, and Joe had his own team to consider. So, he went through the motions and made his presentation. He summed up the many ways in which his proposal would benefit the client.

And then he skipped lunch and left.

He was washing up in the men's room when another figure slipped in. 'Oh, there you are,' said Frank. 'I was looking for you all over. Will you be personally supervising the project?'

'Yes,' said Joe brusquely. 'I would have been,' he added quickly to let Frank know that he knew the project was dead. Joe was a big boy now and could take his lumps and move on, but the molten ball of lead still remained.

To his surprise, Frank grabbed his hand and pumped his arm up and down. 'How wonderful,' said Frank. 'This means we'll be working together again. I'll recommend that we give the contract to your firm. Can you start next month?'

Frank took a bewildered Joe to lunch, and they sat at a private table. 'It's so nice to run into you again like this,' said Frank and he seemed to be sincere. 'I admired you right through school. I could kick a pigskin sphere, hit a hard red ball with a piece of wood, but you…you could really understand math and physics and make them come alive.'

'Yeah,' said Joe, both sceptical and bitter. 'But maybe it's time I asked—how come you never wanted to be seen with me outside school?'

Frank did not pick up on the depth of emotion in Joe's question. 'I was ashamed,' he confessed sheepishly. 'I thought if you knew how shallow my friends were, and how frivolously we wasted time, you wouldn't want to work with me again. Remember the time you explained Fermat's Enigma? I really wanted to know more, but those idiots couldn't understand the beauty of what you had just laid out. I wanted to be more like you, but I just didn't have what it takes. The theories and formulae never sang to me as they did to you.

'I went to a lot of trouble to engineer a weekend just for the two of us. I was hoping you would explain some of the exercises you were working on that were far outside the syllabus, but you turned me down. I can understand that you didn't want to hang around with someone so far behind you,' continued Frank wistfully, 'but after all these years, it still hurts a little.'

The molten ball of lead said goodbye and disappeared.

Joe reached out and clasped Frank's hand. 'Let's make this project a home run,' he said, his eyes moist.

What happened in your past matters a little. The stories you tell yourself about what happened to you in your past matter a great deal.

Don't be like Joe.

Don't tell yourself stories that cement your past into a disagreeable mess. What happened in your past matters a little. The stories you tell yourself about what happened to you in your past matter a great deal.

Choose wisely.

36

THIS POWERFUL TECHNIQUE WILL MAKE YOU THE MASTER OF ALL SITUATIONS

We are buffeted every day as we go about our lives. Our desires are not fulfilled, our expectations are not met, our best-laid plans unravel and we feel as if we are wading through molasses. We are stuck. Or we *feel* stuck.

Shanna blearily rubbed her eyes. She had already hit the snooze button twice. Now she had to get out of bed.

She was a fourth-year associate with a top, white-shoe law firm. Her reviews were great. She was on track to make partner in three years.

She should have felt on top of the world. Few of her law school classmates were doing as well as she was, and two of her best friends had been laid off. One had accepted a position at a tiny, three-attorney, we-handle-any-legal-problem firm, and the other was still looking.

But she felt awful. The partner she was working with, who was crucial to her rise, was making insistent passes at her. She had just broken up with her boyfriend—a man she had planned to marry and have children with.

Her father was in the early stages of dementia, and it was progressing much more rapidly than she expected.

And her car, her brand-new BMW convertible, was constantly breaking down. Every warning light on the dashboard would light up and a peremptory voice would tell her to take it to the dealer right away. She had already been to the dealer twice.

The mental chatter we entertain are responsible for all our feelings of being overwhelmed and anxious.

In my programmes, I stress that the mental models we use and the mental chatter we entertain are responsible for all our feelings of being overwhelmed and anxious. If we make appropriate changes in these models, the problems simply vanish. It may take a few—or perhaps more than a few—attempts to get the hang of it, but then it will transform your life.

This is true.

But most of us need a lot of help to identify the errant mental models and the changes we need to make.

Here is a general-purpose solution. Think of it as a can of WD-40. You can use WD-40 to fix a wide range of problems, from a squeaky sliding door to a stuck water valve. My similarly versatile solution is to convert whatever situation you are facing, the one that you resent and is causing you stress, into a game.

You get to decide the rules.

The fun part of a game is playing it. Winning is nice but not mandatory. The playing is what makes it enjoyable and enables you to grow.

This does require you to step outside yourself and view your life as a movie in which you are starring. The script is constantly changing, and you are the one rewriting it.

This strategy enables Shanna to watch her interaction with the partner dispassionately. Should she go to Human Resources? Should she send a stronger signal that she does not appreciate his advances? Should she let him know that she has mentioned some of his trespasses to others in the firm? Would he be shrewd enough to recognize that these others could be deposed to provide contemporaneous corroboration of inappropriate conduct and sexual harassment?

Many avenues open up to Shanna once she adopts this line of thinking and being. She cannot reverse or slow her father's dementia. But she can let him know how much he means to her. She can use the limited time they have together to have deeper conversations. She can bid him goodbye—in her head—and come to terms with the knowledge that his cage of flesh will soon disintegrate.

I get pushback when I advocate this.

This is not a game, I am told. This is *real life*.

You cannot be casual about what is happening and what you do. There are *consequences*.

I hear you. But you are wrong. Life *can* be a game. In fact, it is only when you play it as a game that you can truly enjoy it.

And whether life is a game or not is a *decision* you make. It happens between your ears.

Games also have consequences. You accept them. Ditto in life. If you let doom and gloom envelope you because you think they are real, then you live in quiet desperation. But if you are playing a game skilfully and you accept the outcome of the game, whose rules you have written, then life becomes a blast. An adverse event simply means that you have lost that particular game and it's time to move on to the next one.

Think about what I have just proposed. Don't reject it. Try it out in *your* life.

There will be changes. They will be profound, and they will be for the better.

37

MAKING LIFE EFFORTLESS AND JOYFUL

Kodo Sawaki Roshi was a well-known Zen master who passed away a few decades ago. He was uncompromising in his teachings and used vivid examples. I remember a story he narrated in which carts in Manchuria were pulled by giant dogs.

The driver would dangle slabs of meat in front of the dog's noses, and they would pull the cart as they strove to reach the dripping flesh.

Even so do you live your lives, he admonished.

The truth of it struck home like a hammer blow—we are unhappy because we can see no further than our noses.

When I first heard this story, I was a young graduate striving to get ahead, get promoted and achieve, achieve, achieve.

I never asked *why* I was striving so hard.

Sawaki Roshi stressed that when we expend all our energy and time in trying to satisfy our 'ordinary-person hopes', we waste our lives and a golden opportunity.

It took me a long time to realize that he was not saying that one should not strive. He *was* saying that the striving itself should be transmuted so that it serves a higher purpose.

Take a mother caring for her child with a cold.

On one level, she is helping the child to blow his nose and

feeding him nourishing soup. Certainly, she wants the child to get well, and perhaps she knows she will be able to sleep better when the child does not wake her up by sniffling and coughing.

On another level, she is helping shape a citizen of the future who will contribute to society and propagate the family name and perhaps bring peace to her forbears. On still another level, she is fulfilling her unique path in life. This may have been shaped by culture, and she may or may not have accepted this consciously.

When you act with awareness, you are mindfully conscious of all the different levels from which you are acting.

When you act with awareness, you are mindfully conscious of all the different levels from which you are acting. You are striving, but you are also working on yourself and serving as an example and inspiration to others who come into your purview.

When you become aware of these levels, who you are changes and what you do changes as a consequence.

Life itself becomes easy. You are still the dog pulling to get at the meat, but all sense of striving and effort drops away. You see that you did not work hard to achieve all the good things in your life. Instead, you allowed them to appear. You also allowed the misfortunes to come, and you will now withdraw your permission and banish them. You *don't* have to work hard and use constant willpower and rigid discipline to produce extraordinary outcomes.

Life becomes easy, effortless and joyous.

38

ACHIEVING PHENOMENAL RESULTS WITHOUT STRUGGLE

Here is how most of us live life: We set a goal for ourselves and then take appropriate action to reach that goal. When things do not go our way, we work harder. We put our 'nose to the grindstone' and try to remember that 'when the going gets tough, the tough get going'. Our lives are full of struggle as we total up our accomplishments.

This is just the nature of life, right?

Well, maybe not.

In *The Surrender Experiment*, Michael Alan Singer describes a phase in his life when he spent virtually all his time in deep meditation because he became tired of his own mental chatter.* His description of his life during this phase is eerily similar to that of Indian sage Ramana Maharshi, who simply meditated in the cavernous rooms of the many-level temple at Tiruvannamalai.

Singer was in a doctoral programme in economics at the University of Florida and had to take three exams. He registered

---

*Michael Singer, *The Surrender Experiment*, Harmony, New York, 2015, pp. 60–62.

to take the two that he was somewhat prepared for. Somehow, he got registered for all three, though, and he had not done a stitch of work for his public finance exam. He was tempted to withdraw, but he was experimenting with surrendering to the universe rather than imposing his will on it. He decided to take the exam, thinking that any resulting failure could help in his struggle to vanquish his ego.

On the day before the exam, he picked up his main public finance textbook and read three sections at random. He repeated this the next morning and left to take his exam, fully expecting to fail and fully at peace with it because he was sure he would drop out of his PhD programme to devote himself full-time to spiritual practice.

There were six questions on the exam, and he was required to answer three. Three of the six dealt with the topics that he had briefly studied. He received an 'A' on the exam and even got a commendation from the dean on his exemplary performance.

Do you really have to impose your will, with all the pain it involves and the drama it creates, on the universe to make things happen the way you want them to?

Here is a scary thought: Do you really have to impose your will, with all the pain it involves and the drama it creates, on the universe to make things happen the way you want them to?

Or can you learn to set aside your oh-so-strong preferences and let a greater wisdom guide you effortlessly through life?

Don't rush to answer this question, and don't force it. This is deep, so think about it and let the answer emerge gradually.

39

IF I COULD JUST GET THEM TO CHANGE

With my personal coaching clients, one theme has surfaced many times. Come to think of it, it is also prevalent in the lives of my friends and relatives. Most of us get stuck in the loop of trying to fix the people in our lives, and this desire almost guarantees failure. But does that mean we should stop? The following examples may better illustrate this dilemma.

A busy attorney is scaling new professional heights, but his son is investigating controlled substances and has had several brushes with the law. The lawyer knows that if he could get his son to change, life would be perfect.

An entrepreneur is grappling with a key-employee issue. The employee in question is brilliant and gets the job done. But he is also brusque and alienates everyone—including, unfortunately, clients. If only the entrepreneur could get his problem-hire to adjust that negative personality trait…

A senior executive works long hours. When he gets home, he just wants to put his feet up and relax and watch some junk on the idiot box. He was once a dutiful father, chauffeuring his children to various activities. Now that they have left the house, he feels entitled to his relax-time. But his wife wants to go out for dinner every night and invites persons he finds intolerable. If only he could get her to lay off and let him be…

A woman with a strong sense of propriety has a beautiful, almost perfectly trained dog. But he insists on latching on to the trousers of male visitors and his sharp teeth have left many holes. If only she could get the dog to modify his behaviour…

We are all stuck in the same rut.

We are all trying to fix someone—children, spouses, parents, siblings, relatives, colleagues, bosses, vendors, subordinates and even pets. Think about how you have held your well-being hostage to the behaviour of others. Someone does something you don't want them to do, and you punish yourself by becoming miserable.

They are who they are.

You can try to change them, but success is not guaranteed and failure is likely.

Remember that the hunchback is oblivious to his own crook as he notes those of others.

Accept this gracefully. You also are who you are. Try to make changes in yourself, and remember that the hunchback is oblivious to his own crook as he notes those of others.

Does this mean that you do not try to induce positive change—or what you consider to be positive change—in others? Of course not. It simply means that when you fail, and this will happen often, you do not let it affect your equanimity.

People are different from one another for a reason. Learn to accept and celebrate that difference.

40

WHY YOUR NEW YEAR'S RESOLUTIONS FAIL

We all want to make changes in our life. We want to be thinner, tell funnier jokes, have more money and be famous. We even know, or think we know, how to do it. The problem lies in the actual doing.

How many times—and likely on your birthday or New Year's Day—have you told yourself that, from now on, your life will be different? That you will eat healthier food, quit smoking, stop procrastinating and exercise regularly?

We all want to make changes in our life. We want to be thinner, tell funnier jokes, have more money and be famous.

Be honest, now! How long did your resolutions last?

The reason you—and most people—fail repeatedly is because we try to bring about profound change in ourselves by an act of will. We determine that we *will* stop smoking, that we *will* go to the gym and work out, and so on.

Every time you try to bring about change by an effort of will, you do violence to yourself. Odds are good that you will not succeed. Even if you do, there is a good chance that there will be unintended side effects that you do not care for.

So, for example, you might stop smoking cold turkey but eat too much and put on weight.

There is a better way to bring about behavioural change that sticks. There is a surefire way to change your habits. You do it by systematically examining the mental models you hold, that cause you to see the world the way you do, and by making changes in them. As you do this, you literally *become* a different person, and the change you seek happens effortlessly as a by-product.

Here is an example of how this works in practice.

A good friend would get all steamed up about traffic when he came to visit me. He lived about 2 hours away, and there were frequent traffic jams at the bridges he had to cross. He would also bemoan the fact that he 'never had time' to meditate.

In Zen tradition there is something called 'walking meditation', in which you walk slowly and mindfully and bring your focus back to each step when your mind wanders. I suggested that he experiment with 'driving meditation'.

There was a quick flip in his worldview. Traffic jams went instantly from being a horrible and unwanted part of his life, to being an opportunity to practise mindfulness. He would breathe deeply and keep his attention on inhaling, all the way in and all the way out. Breathe in, breathe out. Breathe in, breathe out. A sense of peace would wash over him and pervade his body, and it persisted even after his journey was over.

He started looking forward to getting stuck in his next traffic snarl!

Here is another example, and it is both funny and instructive. Four young boys, who ate at the same table in a nursery school, would not drink their milk. Cajoling, scolding, reasoning and bribing did not work. They just would not drink their milk.

Inspiration struck the class teacher, and she seated another boy at their table—a boy who ate his food and looked around for more. The very first day he arrived, he drank his milk and seeing that the others had not drunk theirs, reached out for one of their glasses and drank it. Then he took a second one. The two remaining boys grabbed their respective glasses of milk and held them tightly.

The same thing repeated the next day except that, this time, the newcomer was able to grab three glasses of milk in addition to his own. The boys complained to the teacher about the behaviour of the new boy.

She was nonchalant. 'If you don't want him to drink your milk, then perhaps you should drink it before he can grab it,' she told them.

They all started drinking their milk, and fast! There was no dawdling.

The teacher was able to engineer a shift in the boys' mental model about milk. It went from 'I can do what I want with it, and I can take my time with this' to 'If I don't drink it fast, I will lose it'. And she was able to do this with no struggle.

You may not be able to make such a sudden and complete turnround, but the principle is very solid. Examine the mental models behind the 'suffering' that you are enduring and make appropriate changes.

You will find that you are different, and your life is different.

41

THE QUESTION YOU NEVER ASK CAN SET YOU FREE

We are inquisitive creatures. We want to know what's for dinner and whether we will get promoted and whether our kid will get into Harvard. We don't hesitate to ask questions—lots of questions—but there is one question we do not even think to ask. That is a pity, because asking it could take you on the path to complete freedom.

Curiosity is regarded as a virtue.

Most of our scientific discoveries came about because someone was curious about something. Curiosity led to great discoveries in electricity and magnetism, when Ben Franklin tied a key to a kite and sent it up in a thunderstorm to be hit by lightning.

The overwhelming majority of us ask questions about stuff outside us. We want to make sense of the world we observe.

We can make enormous progress in our well-being if we ask questions about stuff *inside* us.

And here is a great question with which to start:

Why do we need—ever-so-strongly need—the events of our life to be a particular way?

Think about your rigid expectations of life.

You probably don't think you have rigid expectations, but you do. Oh, yes, you do.

You want to be promoted at work and get regular increases in your pay cheque. You want your business to flourish and revenues to increase dramatically. You want your children to be happy, your food to be delicious, your spouse to be caring and your dog to quickly do its thing outside. And you strive mightily to make the world conform to the way you want it to be.

You are troubled when things don't work out the way you would like them to. You redouble your efforts to make the world conform to your desires.

Why is it not all right—or even satisfying—for life to be just the way it is or for it to unfold the way it does without your ever-so-desperate machinations? It is because there is fear in you. You have bought into the if–then model, and it is running your life.

Why is it not all right—or even satisfying—for life to be just the way it is or for it to unfold the way it does without your ever-so-desperate machinations?

Thus, *if* you get promoted, *then* you will be happy. *If* your partner behaves the way you like, *then* you will be happy. And you try and try and try to shape the universe to conform to the way you want it to be.

You don't have control. You've never had control. You never will have control.

And when you come face-to-face with your lack of control, you become afraid.

Think of a time in your life when something happened that you really did not want to happen. Perhaps, you even went out of your way to avoid it. More than likely, it caused a great deal of turmoil in your life at that time.

Now that you have the advantage of hindsight, can you see that it was no big deal?

That is equally true of what you are facing today. Try to gently let go of your preferences—your ever-so-strong preferences.

Say, you really want to be promoted to head of your department. But someone else gets that position. Instead of being agitated and bent out of shape by this, can you simply accept that 'this happened' and continue to enjoy each day?

This does *not* mean that you do not try your level best to rearrange the world to suit your preferences.

It *does* mean that you explicitly recognize that you do not have control and may not succeed in your aim, even if you exert prodigious effort. And you are okay with that.

If you succeed, fantastic.

If you do not succeed, fantastic.

You simply do not allow the success or failure of your endeavours to affect your equanimity and well-being.

Then every day becomes a blast.

42

TO THINK DIFFERENTLY, START WITH INTENTION

In an earlier chapter, I tell you that the way to experience a quantum leap in your life begins with thinking differently. This means that you become aware of the many ways you have been conditioned to view the world and your role in it. Sometimes, this awareness is painful. This conditioning comes from many sources—parents, teachers, siblings, relatives, coaches, friends, media, entertainment sources and so on.

The way to experience a quantum leap in your life begins with thinking differently.

Thinking differently will frequently lead you to act differently, and these divergent actions sometimes lead to great material success. When Fred Smith conceived what would become Federal Express, many conventional thinkers assured him that no one would pay many dollars for a service offered by the US Postal Service for a quarter.

Let's now examine the intent behind your actions. This is what truly determines whether or not you progress spiritually, and find true meaning and purpose in what you do.

I would like you to prosper mightily. Certainly, in material terms—money, power, fame, health and more—but also spiritually. Let's move to a deeper level.

I would like you to be radiantly alive as you go through your day and be filled with a deep sense of purpose. I describe such an ideal life in my manifesto. To get there, you have to pay attention to what you think and do, but also to *why* you do so. Let me explain with an example.

One of my students worked at a prestigious consulting firm. There were days when she disliked her job and even more days when she hated it. Finally, she quit to start her own freelance consulting practice.

The fear set in right away.

Would she be able to get clients? Could she make a go of it? Would she be able to make enough to meet her expenses and someday replace the high income she had?

The first few months were hard. She did odd projects that were 'beneath' her but brought in some cash.

And then, she came across a serious corporate prospect. There was much back and forth, but they finally agreed on a price and she sent in a proposal for them to sign.

She was anxious. This was make-or-break for her—in her mind—and would ensure financial security for at least a year.

She was literally dancing with joy when she met me later that week. 'I got it,' she shouted happily, waving the printout of the email she'd received.

I looked at it. The prospect said that he would be delighted to work with her and suggested settling for a figure that was 10 per cent below what she had quoted.

He also wanted some additional stuff done and said that this was no big deal considering the size of the contract.

He wanted to begin immediately and asked to meet the following Monday.

I looked at her bubbling smile and asked how she felt.

'Fantastic,' she replied. She had been fully prepared to offer the lower figure as a concession if the prospect came back to negotiate. That it was now a done deal seemed incredible, after days of worry and uncertainty.

I advised her to turn it down and email the client that she would have loved to work with him but could not accept his terms.

She looked at me as if I had suddenly sprouted horns, and we talked about it at length.

And then, she did as I suggested.

The client came back for further talks. Eventually, they settled on the figure quoted in the proposal and he agreed to pay for the additional work he wanted.

'Professor Rao, you are brilliant,' she gushed. 'This is a perfect example of using scarcity to create perceived value. I was just too scared to do it. Thanks so much for pushing me.'

Well-documented research shows that people want what they cannot have. So, if you dangle something attractive before someone and then 'induce scarcity', the person on the receiving end is much more likely to buy.

Mediocre marketers use lazy calls to action such as 'supplies are limited'. Smarter ones use specific claims like 'only two seats left' or the ubiquitous '18 people are looking at this deal right now; two seats are available'.

These tactics work. That's why they are used so widely.

Let's dig deeper and go into intent.

My student could have done what she did from the space of: 'I think he is just negotiating. He cannot find anyone else to do this project in the time frame he needs. So, if I hold firm and make him think that he will "lose" me, the scarcity effect will kick in and I will get my price. Let me go for it.'

This is legal and ethical, and makes her a smart businessperson. And many would be happy with the outcome and think no more about it.

Alternatively, my student could have done it from the space of: 'I want to serve this client, but I cannot give my best if he dictates the terms. If I agree to the lower price and his conditions, there will be other demands made and I will resent this, and it will affect the quality of my work. Let me decline and make this clear to him. If I lose the project, then so be it. I only want to work with clients who understand what I stand for.'

This is also legal and ethical and leaves her in a much better emotional domain.

These two viewpoints are not completely distinct, they overlap. And as my student confessed, she was coming from a mixture of both perspectives.

That's okay.

What's important is that you recognize your intent. Be as close to the second viewpoint as you can be. Don't be a sophisticated manipulator of people—be an authentic helper. Don't get so enamoured with the outcome you desire that you are too quick to make compromises. Take your time, and make sure that in your head, you are charting a win-win situation. You get to decide what is win-win, and you also face consequences if your prospect sees it differently. And you accept whatever transpires with equanimity.

The actions are the same and, most likely, the outcomes will be better. And you will feel a whole lot better about yourself, and get closer to the life I describe in the manifesto for my programme.

43

SOMETHING BETTER THAN HOPE

Faith, hope and charity are celebrated in the New Testament book of First Corinthians. These are the three great virtues we are enjoined to cultivate. Let's look at hope.

We have been indoctrinated into the belief that hope is a wonderful virtue to inculcate. There are tales galore of persons, in severely adverse circumstances, who survived because they had hope.

We support those close to us by admonishing them not to lose hope. We define 'losers' in our society as persons who have given up hope. I invite you to consider that this approach, which has undoubtedly helped many, may still be flawed.

Built into the very fabric of hope is the notion that tomorrow will be better. We ignore today because it is too problematic, and live in the expectation that tomorrow will solve all our problems.

There will always be another tomorrow. That, in fact, is the stirring conclusion of *Gone with the Wind.*

Here is the catch: When we fixate on what will come or could come tomorrow, we dismiss the present. We even denigrate it.

But today is all you have. It is all you will ever have.

When you are busy imagining the many ways in which the future will be better, you are ignoring the gift that the present has for you.

When you are busy imagining the many ways in which the future will be better, you are ignoring the gift that the present has for you. And it is a munificent gift.

Our mental chatter leads us to conclude that our present is terrible and needs to be altered. It is the incessant voice in our head that insists we should change our circumstances. It is this voice that drives us in our quest for more.

We want more money, a bigger house, a better spouse, more accomplished children, more fame and power and prestige. More, more, always more.

And hope is the handmaiden of this urge, feeding it with the notion of possibility. It makes us unhappy in the present and teaches us to live for—and in—the future. And we forget that we can only be joyful *now*!

I get great pushback when I speak about this in public forums.

I am asked if I advocate not planning for the future, and abandoning striving to make oneself better. Of course not. You *should* strive to grow, materially and spiritually. In fact, it is your *obligation* to do so. But do so with a sense of joy and gratitude. Do so with the knowledge that planning for tomorrow happens today. That the actions you undertake to bring about that future are taken in the present.

This way you enjoy each day, and it is complete in and of itself. Tomorrow will be the same when it arrives.

You don't work and strive in the hope that there will be a superior tomorrow.

You work and strive because the working and striving itself

are providing you with the nourishment you need for your growth.

Tomorrow will turn out the way it turns out, and you are fine with it. Today is all you have. Make full use of it!

Try living this way. You may be surprised at how light and cheerful you feel.

44

WHAT A BABY KNOWS THAT YOU DON'T

We have an insidious habit that plays havoc in our lives. You do it. I do it. We all do it. And it hurts us in ways we don't even recognize. This habit is that of holding on to past hurt—thereby, allowing it to continue harming us.

Many speakers say that we should pay attention to everyone who crosses our path because each person is unique, and each person can teach us something if only we are open and receptive.

Perhaps.

Today, I would like to you to consider what you can learn from a baby. And this is a lesson that will instantly improve your life. Consider Sasha.

> It was a crowded party, and Sasha tried her best to avoid Denise, but some interfering busybody grabbed her hand and introduced her to Amanda—who, of course, was Denise's friend and promptly called her over.
>
> Sasha and Denise had gone to the same high school. They were even friends of a sort.
>
> But then, Sasha ran for class president and was instantly attacked for being 'too cozy' with the administration. It was alleged that she shared her

campaign platform with the principal and modified it based on his ideas. He, in turn, appointed her to be the school representative for outside events and thus in a position to dole out patronage positions to her supporters. Many felt that she had obtained an unfair advantage.

Denise did not back her up. In fact, she campaigned for Sasha's opponent. They had words. And they never spoke again.

And now Denise was looking inquiringly at Sasha. 'How are you doing?' she asked cordially.

'Well enough, now that I don't have any traitors in my camp,' Sasha returned tartly.

There was another unpleasant surprise waiting for her the next day.

Sasha had just been hired at a new company, and it turned out that Denise was her boss.

She wondered if she should quit before she was fired.

She could have cried.

We carry around our hurts, resentments, grievances and feelings of being slighted. This is a rock on our heads, and it weighs heavy.

We carry around our hurts, resentments, grievances and feelings of being slighted. This is a rock on our heads, and it weighs heavy.

I know a few people who take pride in never forgetting that they have been wronged by someone, and they consider this a strength. They also look to get even. They are stuck in the past. And every so often, as happened to Sasha, that past will bite you on the nose if you don't let go of it.

What does all this have to do with babies?

Look at a baby happily gurgling as he drinks from his bottle.

Now, take the bottle away.

His face becomes red as he wails mightily, and waves his hands and feet in frustration. There is no doubt that this is one enraged wee being.

Now, give him the bottle back. In seconds, he is back to drinking and gurgling happily. The baby experiences anger and frustration to its fullest extent, and then he lets it go! The problem with us is that we are pretty good at doing the experiencing, but lousy at letting it go.

Think of the interactions you have with the people in your life. The ghosts of what happened in the past are always there, colouring your views and attitudes and expectations.

You are stuck in the past and you mentally imprison the other person as well by being so. But the one you harm the most is you.

Try to put your rock down.

45

HOW THE **** DO YOU LET IT GO?

I had a lot of work to do, but I met with Felicity because she was quite insistent. She was crying, and by the looks of her red, puffy face, I suspected that she had been sobbing earlier.

She had just broken up with her boyfriend. She was 'ready' and he was not, so they decided to go their separate ways after a tempestuous fight. She had a history of pairing up with individuals who wouldn't commit, so she had been to this town before.

But this time, it hit her much harder than usual. They had been together for three years, and she was pushing 40 and not sure she could go through another such cycle again.

I listened sympathetically and was about to tell her to 'let it go' when she exploded. Her mother, doubtless with the best of intentions, had told her to 'let it go' and her best friend, commiserating, had also suggested that she 'let it go'.

'Do you think I want to hold on to it?' She was sobbing now, with no pretence of control. 'Just how the **** do I "let it go"?'

A good question.

In fact, an excellent question.

We all walk around weighed down by mistakes from our

We all walk around weighed down by mistakes from our past.

past. Tennis players remember how they double-faulted when serving for the match, and relive that moment over and over again. They also recreate it. Divorces get nasty because each partner remembers every unpleasant remark the other made.

Think back over your life.

How much historical junk are you lugging around?

Do you dread meeting with your boss because he has slighted you in public before, and you don't want it to happen again?

Does the residue of your past experiences colour your feelings toward your spouse, child, parent, relative or friend?

Do your many errors of omission and commission bedevil you and induce fear, worry and sleeplessness?

Let it go. Let *all* of it go.

Here's *how* to let it go.

The first step is to separate yourself from your persistent and painful thoughts. Become aware of your mental chatter. Recognize that it is just mental chatter.

My former student was crying because she remembered the many wonderful times she and her ex had together and how beautiful the future was going to be, except it suddenly wasn't going to be.

It was just a thought in her head.

Thoughts in your head are both supremely powerful, and utterly inconsequential.

They are powerful because you identify with them, and that arouses emotions and impacts everything from intentions to physical actions and bodily reactions. They are inconsequential because you can refuse to identify with them, and then they have no power over you at all.

Imagine that it is a beautiful day. You are lying on a grassy knoll, looking up at the clouds in the sky. You shut your eyes for a few minutes and look up again. Those clouds are gone, but new ones have appeared.

You can admire the clouds—both the ones above you and the ones that have gone.

Thoughts are like the clouds in the sky. They come and they go. They cannot drag you down with them if you remain aware.

Felicity was able to see that she had built up an entire future life and fallen in love with it. And now that life was not going to be. But it was all a thought in her head and she could, if she tried, see that it was all a thought in her head.

I advised her not to go for distractions like movies, calling friends or consuming alcohol.

Instead, I encouraged her to sit and watch her thoughts as if she were in a theatre watching a movie. I advised her to feel the pain and move to a position of observing herself feeling the pain.

This is not easy, but it can be done.

Felicity did it. She slipped many times but she picked herself up each time, going back into witness mode and recognizing the sandcastles she had built.

There is absolutely nothing wrong with building sandcastles, but don't get so attached to them that when one crumbles it tosses you for a loop. Enjoy the building process, but don't obsess over the outcome.

The only way you can do that is to become a witness and observe those darn thoughts.

Within a month, Felicity was able to talk about him without breaking down and then he became a bittersweet memory with no emotional drain.

That is how you let it go.

46

DON'T MAKE THE MISTAKE I MADE

Sometimes our life gets too busy, and we let things slide. Here is a cautionary tale and a lesson from my life.

Near the end of the year, I made a bunch of phone calls but reached few of the persons I wanted to. Companies were slowing down, and executives were more concerned with holiday plans than business. My wife was in California visiting our daughter, so I was holding down the fort in New York and taking care of my mother-in-law, the most good-natured and undemanding elderly relative you can hope to find.

As I was acknowledging the many blessings in my life, I remembered a friend of mine. We had known each other for more than three decades and met socially many times in the early days.

Then geography intervened. He moved west, and I moved east. I used to joke that New York was close to the largest toxic dump in the world—a place called New Jersey. As a new resident of that state, he did not agree.

We met for lunch two or three times a year. He would drive more than two-thirds of the way, braving both river crossings.

Sometimes the trip would take him 2 hours each way, but he never complained or suggested that perhaps I could travel closer to him the next time.

We had deep conversations. We discussed family, philosophy, business and where we were headed in our lives.

When I was passing through a turbulent phase, he found his own gentle way of supporting me. He was unfailingly encouraging and frequently gave me examples of how something I had told him made a big impact on his life. He was not lying, nor was he flattering me. He was trying to get me to expand my thinking so I could reach more people through my writing and public events. He was reassuring me that I was okay.

We were supposed to meet one day, but something came up so I asked if we could reschedule. He was leaving for an international trip, so we agreed to meet after his return.

He emailed me when he got back, and we scheduled but I cancelled again. He sent me alternate dates, but none of them worked for me. He called me to set something up in real time. I was in a bit of a time crunch with several projects coming to a head simultaneously for me, so I asked if we could meet in six months.

Of course, he readily agreed. He emailed me again in a few months and I meant to reply, but somehow his message got lost in my inbox and I never responded.

He called me from Florida where he was vacationing. We had a brief conversation because I was interrupted by another call that took priority. We agreed to meet on his return.

I dropped the ball again.

I was in London on a business trip. I came across his old email and determined that we absolutely should get together. It had now been more than two years since our last meeting.

The following day, my wife called to inform me that my

friend had passed away peacefully. She wanted to know if I would be back for the funeral service.

Pancreatic cancer moves swiftly. His illness was already advanced when he had called me from Florida. I keep wondering if he would have told me about it if I had not abruptly ended our call. And I kick myself for not knowing, for not being there for him, even as he always made time for me when I needed it.

He was gone before I could say goodbye or let him know how much I valued his friendship.

You mean to. But something always intervenes, and you resolve to do it tomorrow. Sometimes tomorrow never comes.

Life always encroaches on us. The 'urgent' rides roughshod over us and sidelines the 'important'. There is someone in your life who is important to you. You wish them well and love them dearly. But you have not made the phone call or sent them the email to let them know this. You want to. You mean to. But something always intervenes, and you resolve to do it tomorrow.

Sometimes tomorrow never comes.

So, reach out to that person *today*. Draft and send that email. Make the phone call. Don't set yourself up for unending regret. You will bring joy to their life.

And to yours.

47

THE INVISIBLE THREADS THAT BIND YOU

Sometimes, things are not what they seem. I encountered this recently when I stopped by a friend's place when her in-laws were visiting. They seemed like an amiable couple, and they also seemed to like my friend. They gave her an expensive outfit that, to my untutored eyes, seemed to be a really generous gift.

Later, when they had left, my friend made a disparaging remark and I chided her for ingratitude. She laughed good-naturedly. 'If you knew what was really happening, you would have used a lot stronger language than I did,' she remarked.

My interest was piqued. I wanted to know what was really happening.

'They just put another rope around me,' she explained.

It turned out that the gift they gave carried a heavy burden. They expected her to wear it when they came to visit. They remembered every present they gave her and were not above asking her why she never wore 'that wonderful outfit' or carried 'that adorable bag' they had given her years ago. They even asked her husband, their son, if she was upset with them because she did not use the gifts they so thoughtfully and lovingly got her.

'They think they are being kind, but I feel smothered,' said my friend. 'They even get upset if I am confused about whether some gewgaw they got me was for my birthday or an anniversary. I have enough going on in my life without having to remember what they gave me and when. I don't want that crap anyway.'

It struck me that we are all, in our own ways, guilty of exactly the same failing her parents-in-law had.

Do you remember how many times you have invited your neighbour over for coffee but he never reciprocated?

Do you keep mental note of who picked up the tab when you went out to a restaurant?

Do you keep letting a friend know that you have 'forgiven' her for the way she wronged you?

Don't hang on to what you have given away.

Do you lay guilt trips on your children for not calling or visiting?

Do you expect to be thanked profusely for the special-occasion gift you gave your close friends?

These are all invisible threads that we attach to the stuff we think we have given away. These threads weave a net that traps both us and the persons on whom we bestow our largesse.

When you give a gift, whether it is a physical item, an act of service or something intangible like forgiveness, let it go! Even the expectation of a thank-you can become a burden.

What feeds you, nourishes you and makes you grow is the ability to be of service to all and sundry. You help because you are able to. Don't dilute this powerful mechanism with your expectations.

Don't hang on to what you have given away.

48

PUT DOWN THE SUITCASE

Tiny mental habits niggle at us and wear us down. They sap our energy, and contribute to the tension and anxiety that is always with us.

Here is what you can do about it.

I went to meet my teacher—my guru, actually—before I came to the US for my doctoral studies. My mind was troubled—it always was in those days—and I had many questions. I am sure he addressed them, but I don't recall what he said.

I do remember the gentle admonition he gave me: 'Srikumar, the train is powerful enough to carry you and your suitcases. You do not have to carry the suitcases on your head. Put them down.'

His words were vaguely comforting, but I had no clue about what a profound teaching he had just shared with me.

I do now.

Every day we carry a suitcase on our heads. Every day we carry a burden we should not be carrying, one the train can carry for us. We feel fear and anxiety and nervousness and self-loathing and insecurity. We think we are not as good as others think we are, and we are afraid everyone will soon find this out.

We worry that what we have spent so many years accumulating will be stripped from us. We fear the global forces that scream at us from news headlines and the impact they will have on society, and eventually on us.

These are the suitcases we are carrying.

Seriously, when was the last time you were completely okay? When there was truly nothing bothering you or of concern to you?

Most of us cannot remember such a time. We are so used to the suitcases we carry.

We try to fix our internal turbulence by external action. We feel lonely, so we rush about trying to find a companion, even 'the one'. We fear being fired and jobless, so we restrain ourselves at work and try to put our best foot forward and not rock the boat.

How do you put down those darn suitcases?

Start by being aware that you are carrying them!

Watch the stories you tell yourself, how quickly they arise and how rapidly they force you into emotional domains you do not want to inhabit.

Say, you have worked hard on a proposal and submitted it to a client you thought was in the bag. He promised to get back to you by the end of the week but did not. Nor did he get to it the following week. Your phone calls were not returned, and your emails were left unanswered.

Think of how many what-if scenarios you generate. Stuff that you should not have put in the proposal. Stuff that you should have included but did not. Deadlines that could have been made more flexible. And so much more.

And the stories don't end there.

You think of what will happen to your company and you,

your plans for the future and how these may be upended and more.

Just recognize that these ponderings are no more than stories. Once you have truly seen that these stories have no power except what you give them, you begin reclaiming your life.

Stuff happens. Watch it happen and enjoy it. Sometimes you like what happens, and sometimes you don't. Tell yourself stories you can enjoy—even when things that you don't like happen.

Stuff happens. Watch it happen and enjoy it. Sometimes you like what happens, and sometimes you don't.

You go to an expensive restaurant, the service is lousy and the server messes up the orders, switching your dish with someone else's. You can be royally pissed off. Or you can decide that you will not give the server any power to determine how you feel and sit back to enjoy a dish that is strange to you, or less than perfect.

Do this with all the things that bother you each day.

That is how you put down your suitcases.

49

THIS IS WHY YOU SUFFER!

He was a diligent student. He did all the exercises and assignments in my programme and benefitted greatly from them. Then one day, he approached me about a serious problem he had. He was an alcoholic. He had kicked the habit numerous times, but somehow, he always relapsed.

'I know it's bad for me,' he said. 'I know it very clearly, but I just can't stop myself. Can you help me?'

I thought about the numerous persons I know who have participated in Creativity and Personal Mastery over the decades and have expressed something similar to me.

I have my own thorns. I know that salty Indian snacks are bad for me, but I indulge in them anyway.

How about you? Are there things you do that you clearly know are not in your best interest? Like checking your email compulsively? Or being driven by overweening ambition? Or ignoring your family while you climb your career ladder?

Are there things you do that you clearly know are not in your best interest?

Here is some disquieting news for you. The reason you indulge in these self-defeating behaviours is that you *don't* know how much they are harming you. You think you know, but you don't. You just have a vague, nebulous feeling that something may not be the best for you, and that perhaps you shouldn't be doing it.

Imagine, you are walking in the countryside on a path bound by thick hedges on either side. Suddenly you see an out-of-control car careening toward you.

What do you do?

Here's one thing you don't do. You don't seek out a sage and relate your tale of woe to him. 'Oh, holy one, there is a car coming toward me. What should I do? Can you please guide me?'

You go through the nearest hedge instantly. You don't pause to think that this is an impossible task, that it is a thick hedge, that you may get scratched or that your new clothes might get torn.

The reason you do this is because you know—really *know* in a visceral, deep-down way—what will happen to you if the car hits you. If you had an equal degree of clarity about the other stuff in your life, you would not do what you do.

So how do you get that clarity?

Sometimes, you are dragged willy-nilly into a different state of consciousness. Have you ever had someone close to you die unexpectedly?

There was grief, of course, but there was also reflection. A sense that you were far too preoccupied with trivial matters. Quite possibly, you determined to live differently going forward.

And then, of course, you went back to your normal life with its incessant striving—where the rainbow was always over the next hill.

Why can't you retain that sense of clarity?

Because you have been programmed to revert to your unthinking ways.

There is a way to be anchored in your new realization, if you choose to. But, you have to work at it and employ a powerful tool.

That tool is deep reflection. In deep reflection, you consciously bring to mind and meditate on the ramifications of the behaviour that is troubling you. Are you fiercely ambitious to the point that you cannot sleep? Are you consumed by work to the extent that your family is suffering and insomnia stalks you?

Think about the inevitability of death and how 'Scepter and crown / Must tumble down, / And in the dust be equal made / With the poor humble scythe and spade'*. In India, seekers meditate in cremation grounds and graveyards to impress on themselves that life is transitory.

Are you lustful and fixated on sex? Think of the human body and what it is composed of. Blood that pours out of cuts, pus that forms in wounds, bones and excrement and entrails. Can you really be attracted to something so gross?

And as for my alcoholic student? He can reflect on the many artists and thespians who died prematurely from liver failure, and contemplate accomplishments that will not come to be because of his addiction.

Whatever it is that troubles you, there is a deep reflection that can rid you of that programming. This is a very powerful tool. Use it with care.

---

*'Death the Leveller Poem by James Shirley', *PoemHunter.com*, https://tinyurl.com/2dr5vy4u. Accessed on 11 August 2023.

50

A SMOKED-GLASS TABLE AND A LIFE LESSON ON TRANSIENCE

When I got married, I was an executive, but in my head I was a graduate student so my place reflected that. The little furniture I had was mismatched and shabby, and books were everywhere.

My wife and I moved to an apartment, and we needed a dining room set. I saw a picture of one with a smoked-glass table and elegant chairs, and I wanted it. I mean *really* wanted it. My wife would have been satisfied with any number of choices, but I refused them all. Nothing but that smoked-glass table for me.

We bought it. It was expensive, and we scrimped elsewhere.

We moved from an apartment to a starter home, and then added substantially to it to accommodate our growing family. The table came with us and was now in the family room. There were many happy memories of us playing games on it, using it as a snack table during parties and so on.

My son became a serious model builder, and it served as his worktable. He was really good. He won first or second prize in his age group at the International Plastic Modelers Convention in all three categories he entered—aircraft, ships and armoured fighting vehicles. We still have boxes of finely-painted finished models and shelves of awards and plaques.

My son left home years ago to begin clerking for a justice in the Utah Supreme Court. My daughter left more than a decade ago. She is married and runs her own startup. And we have a house full of memories and far too much stuff.

Last week, my wife dragged my unwilling self into a cleaning spree and we packed away my son's model-building gear and tools. The hood and exhaust fan went into storage.

And the smoked-glass table, which now had streaks of paint on the surface? We left it outside a day before the garbage pickup. It was gone the next morning along with the chairs. I hope that whoever took it makes equally happy memories while sitting around it with friends and family.

And that brings me to the life lesson.

Whatever we gather, hoard and cherish is in time and space. And whatever is in time and space will wither and be stripped from us, whether we like it or not. Your baby's first tooth in its own tiny silver casket; your college diploma that represents so much money and time and effort; your elegant clothes; your carefully preserved bottles of fine wine; your cherished mementoes and keepsakes—it's all stuff. Just stuff. And it will all go one day.

Whatever we gather, hoard and cherish is in time and space. And whatever is in time and space will wither and be stripped from us, whether we like it or not.

Think about this. Really think about the impermanence of things.

Nothing lasts forever.

When this seeps into your consciousness, your relationship with the world of things changes. You still use them, but you are not attached to them. They come and they go and that is fine; that is the way it should be.

And you experience a tiny reflection of the freedom that sages have known and extol.

Begin today. Pick up any item you have not used for a year or more. Does it still add value to your life? Or is it clutter that remains to complicate your existence?

If you do not actively want it, get rid of it. Give it away to someone deserving, and you'll find that the joy of doing so considerably overshadows the momentary pang of regret.

51

THE JOURNEY TO REHABILITATION

I found a really great example for a lesson I want to share with you. And I found it by happenstance, when I was not looking. In fact, I was goofing off and watching a movie. It told the story of a destitute family, a moment of loss, and how you create the pain and suffering in your life.

Saroo grew up dirt poor in India. He was very close to his elder brother, Guddu, who would watch out for him and play with him and promise to get him lots of *jelabis*—an Indian sweet—that they were too poor to afford.

Saroo was also close to his mother, who would hug him, cuddle him, feed him and care for him.

When he was five years old, Saroo went to sleep in a stationary train that started up and transported him to Kolkata, more than a thousand miles from home.

Destitute and starving, unable to speak Bengali, the local language, he ended up in an orphanage, where he was adopted by an affluent Australian couple. He was transported to and brought up in Tasmania.

He experienced recurrent flashes from his childhood, and with the help of friends he estimated how long he was on the train and mapped out places that could have been his home. He then spent months visiting these via Google Earth.

Finally, he struck pay dirt and spotted some landmarks he recognized from his childhood. He went to India to meet his birth family. There was a tearful reunion with his mother. And then he asked, 'Where's Guddu?'

It turned out that Guddu had been struck by a train and died the same night he was lost.

Saroo dissolved into tears, and his heartache was palpable.

For the curious, the movie is *Lion*, released in 2016 and directed by Garth Davis. The lesson? It is that the grief he felt was something he manufactured in his head.

Pause to think this through before you push back. Guddu had died nearly three decades earlier. But the sorrow and anguish Saroo felt was today. This agony was created by the way he processed information.

It existed only in his head!

He did not realize that he was creating his own pain. Quite likely, it was involuntary. Possibly, you also are reluctant to accept that Saroo fabricated his grief. Yes, Saroo's emotions were socially appropriate and will not be harmful if he lets them go in good time. But he did make them up. He took a memory, infused it with emotion, mixed it with recent knowledge of past events and felt deep pain.

He took a memory, infused it with emotion, mixed it with recent knowledge of past events and felt deep pain.

You do the same.

Every time you think of an ex or some mistake you made in the past and wince, every time you worry about any event or future that 'could happen', you are manufacturing sorrow and anxiety.

Think about this again and again until you see very clearly that this, in fact, is what you are doing. Recognizing this is the first step on the long journey to rehabilitation.

You indulge in much needless suffering. Stop doing so.

52

A SINGLE QUESTION WILL DRAMATICALLY IMPROVE YOUR LIFE

We are always telling ourselves stories. We ask ourselves questions and then answer them and, as we do so, we also shape our lives.

There is a quick way to vastly improve your life. It is simple, but not easy. All you have to do is sincerely ask a question that begins, 'Do I *really*...?'

When you start asking yourself this one question, you'll begin to see a shift in your quality of life.

Let me explain.

Look inside your closet. I will wager that there are many clothes you have not worn for years and, very likely, will not wear again.

'Do I really want this in my life?'

So, why are they in your closet?

That is because when you were debating what to do with a particular outfit, you asked, 'Is there any conceivable occasion when I may use this?'

And the answer, of course, is 'Yes!'

Now, change the question to 'Do I *really* want this in my life?' What is the worst thing that would happen to you if you gave it away? Not much. It would not make a material difference in your life. So, out it goes and you get more space in your closet.

If you pick up any article in your house and ask, 'Do I *really* want this in my life?' you will be surprised at how much you have that you do not really need. Let go of anything that is not serving you and enriching your life.

This is a great tool for getting rid of clutter.

It is also a great tool for the mind, and this is where the benefits are greatest. This question can give you freedom that you never dreamed of.

Let's say you like watching slasher movies or reading edgy thrillers. This means that, for some time at least, you inhabit a world where crazy, malicious people do horrible things to innocent victims. In this world, violence happens and the 'bad guy' eventually comes to a grisly end.

What does this experience do to *you*? Does it reinforce a world view that violence is the answer? Is this what you truly believe?

Ask yourself sincerely, 'Do I *really* want to go there?' It's okay if you do, for any number of reasons. Just do so consciously and mindfully.

If you do this earnestly, for any length of time, there will be changes in the books you read; the movies you watch; the people you hang out with; the topics of conversation you bring up with the people you hang out with; and much more.

Gradually, your whole life will be transformed for the better and you will feel much more at peace with yourself.

And it all begins with a simple question: 'Do I *really*...?'

53

AN UNSPEAKABLE TRAGEDY

On 25 April 2015, an earthquake of magnitude 7.6 struck Nepal and parts of India. The death toll was more than 10,000, and the number of injured was many times more. It triggered an avalanche on Mt Everest that wiped out the basecamp and killed 19 climbers. Historic buildings, many centuries old, collapsed. Hundreds of thousands were left homeless. As always, the poor were rendered even more destitute. I wanted to contribute to the relief effort but held off.

In the immediate aftermath of such a monumental tragedy, the world wakes up and contributions flood in. But attention soon fades, life intrudes and we move on to our everyday lives and forget. A few weeks later, this tragedy merges with so many others and fades from our attention.

But you cannot pretend that all is fine.

It is precisely at this time that help is most needed. The aid workers have gone, and those who lost loved ones are alone to confront their grief. Those in makeshift camps have to think about where they can go and what to do next.

It is easy to reach out and donate to one of the many organizations that are doing relief work—sometimes yeoman relief work. Let me suggest something different to you—

something that will take more of your time and effort but that will also make it *personal.*

Seek out a specific individual or family that has been affected and contribute directly to that person or family.

We eat regularly at an Indian restaurant near our house, and one of the waiters is Nepali. My wife found out that his home had collapsed, and his mother was crushed. We donated to him directly. There is a unique power in delivering help to a person who needs it.

There are many Nepalis in low-wage jobs in major cities. Make the effort to find out who they are, and identify a specific person who has suffered loss. Contact aid workers who are on the spot, and ask them for names of individuals who have suffered loss.

Some of the relief organizations will cooperate and give you contact information for the persons on the ground. They will undoubtedly be puzzled by your request.

You understand that you are reaching out as a human being to help another human being in his time of trouble. You are putting something of yourself into it, something more than fungible money. It is your time and sweat and effort and care.

There is a difference between donating to a hospital and personally caring for a quadriplegic and wiping the drool from his lips. We are all beset with to-do lists, and they are constantly growing. It is easy to put off such a personal initiative, precisely because it will eat up a significant chunk of your time and you might not get a direct reward.

We like to think of ourselves as selfless. But, are we really? When we hold the door open for someone, we expect a 'thank you' and may even get riled if the person passes through without acknowledgement. If we are kind to our fellow beings, we expect to be appreciated.

Much of the time—not always, but a great deal of the time and perhaps even the vast majority of the time—we are helpful because we get acknowledgement, appreciation, fame and various other types of ego-gratification.

Philanthropy in the US is an intricate charade where the wealthy are wooed and coddled and played up to. Their names are put on buildings, their generosity noted in media and consultants galore make their living coming up with ways to uniquely honour them.

Doubtless, much good comes of this—for example, the New York Public Library System was created through Carnegie's millions. But could the donor have benefitted even more?

Think of instances in your life when you did something that benefitted someone else without any thought of thanks, recognition or acknowledgement you might receive. Only the knowledge that you did something to aid someone else, such as the time you stopped your car and moved a stone off the road so no motorist ran into it. Or when you moved a supermarket shopping cart back to the store, so it no longer blocked a parking spot. Or when you gave a dollar to a street musician, but you also looked into his eyes, acknowledged him as a human being and thanked him for bringing joy into your life.

Think of instances in your life when you did something that benefitted someone else without any thought of thanks, recognition or acknowledgement you might receive.

Can you recall such instances? How many can you recall? These are the bricks on which a fulfilled life is built.

And that is precisely the point.

You are doing this for you. You are the one who will ultimately benefit when you put more of yourself, mindfully and consciously, into the act of reaching out and helping.

Try it.

54

PATHS OF GLORY LEAD BUT TO THE GRAVE

Shah Jahan came in fashionably late, and occupied his cushioned seat atop the intricately carved marble structure on which his throne rested. It was a hot tropical morning, but his heavy robes actually kept him cool and shielded him from the searing wind. His diadem-laden head felt heavy and he refrained from turning his head for fear that his crown would fall. He looked at the pulsing, seething crowd below and instantly they fell to their knees in homage. A far larger crowd had gathered outside the red sandstone walls of his palace.

There was anger in the air, rapidly changing to fear. He was about to help that transformation accelerate. Today was not an ordinary court day. Today, he would let his subjects know what happened when they forgot that he, and he alone, was their divinely appointed ruler.

He leaned forward slightly, to look directly below him. A dozen naked men were there, each held in chains by two burly guards. They were in sorry shape. Many had broken limbs with white bones showing through torn skin. Flesh, charred with branding irons, was suppurating. One man was comatose, with only the chains keeping him upright.

They had all confessed. Under enhanced interrogation from his most skilled intelligence officers, they had given up comrades and exposed the conspiracy. Even now his horsemen were pursuing the one surviving leader. He would soon be captured.

It was time to teach his subjects a lesson they would never forget. He raised his hand.

There was instant silence.

He pronounced the sentences. They would all die the traditional death of traitors, in public. A dozen pits had already been dug in the field outside. They would be buried up to their necks, and then the royal execution elephant, decorated and gaily caparisoned, would stroll through the maidan. Skulls would flatten with a sickening pop while bloodthirsty crowds cheered.

He would not be there. His favourite queen had arranged a special entertainment for him. Her men had finally captured the giant tiger, known as Sher Khan, that had achieved such renown that even he had heard of it. This evening there would be wine and music and dancing girls, as Sher Khan was pitted against his war elephant in a battle to the death.

He looked forward to it. It had been a tiring day.

This is fiction. However, scenes such as this happened with some frequency during the reign of Shah Jahan, the fifth Mughal emperor who is better known as the builder of the Taj Mahal.*

His palace, the Red Fort, was constructed in 1648 and is now a World Heritage Site. At the time, the Mughal Empire held sway over more than 150 million persons and represented nearly a quarter of the world's economy.

The kingdom did not come easily to Shah Jahan. Born Prince Khurram, he was the third son of Emperor Jahangir. Khurram killed his older siblings in fratricidal war to grab the throne. Immediately after his victory, he ordered the execution of his younger brother, Shahryar, and the imprisonment of his father's favourite queen.

Shah Jahan certainly did not foresee that his third son, Aurangzeb, would slay his own brothers to grab the Mughal throne and then imprison him in Agra Fort. Shah Jahan could see the Taj Mahal take shape but would not 'visit' it until he died and was laid to rest beside his wife, Mumtaz Mahal.

The intricately carved marble structure, from which he surveyed his subjects in the royal *darbar*, was now viewed by him from a sorry corner of the castle. Random tourists such like me gape at the Taj Mahal and take selfies.

Think about what you, today, are striving to achieve. Think of the tremendous expenditure of emotional energy, of the pain and suffering, of the hopes and fears. One day, regardless of whether you win or lose, all of it will be equally forgotten and disregarded.

One day, regardless of whether you win or lose, all of it will be equally forgotten and disregarded.

*For more historical fiction accounts of Shah Jahan's reign, see: Rutherford, *The Serpent's Tooth*, Headline Publishing Group, 2013.

Remember the words of Shakespeare in *Hamlet*: 'Imperious Caesar, dead and turn'd to clay, Might stop a hole to keep the wind away.'*

Does this mean that you should stop striving? Not at all. But it does mean that you should be exceedingly careful about *what* you are striving for, and *why* you are striving for it. Recognize that the true value of what you are doing is not the 'success' or 'failure' of your efforts, but the changes these efforts produce in you.

That is the most valuable life lesson for you.

*'The Tragedy of Hamlet, Prince of Denmark', *Shakespeare.mit*, https://tinyurl.com/ykn274sh. Accessed on 11 August 2023.

55

THE LITTLE-KNOWN SECRET TO ACHIEVING INCREDIBLE SUCCESS

I made a mistake when I was young. It took me decades to recognize that I had made it. I will do what I can to make sure you don't make the same error.

What was that mistake?

I'll tell you. But first, let me share some background.

Buddhist sages have exhorted lay followers to practise Dharma and consciously follow a spiritual path. The Indian sage, Shankara, spoke about humanity's endless striving for pleasure, sex and wealth, and how this leads persons astray and away from the path of genuine happiness. St Timothy beseeched everyone to flee youthful passions, pursue righteousness and call on the Lord from a pure heart.

My mother knew about all of them and more. She urged me to read works by the great masters and live by their words.

I wasn't having any of it.

I wanted 'success' now. Far from eschewing worldly gains, I actively pursued them. And I continued to batter my head against brick walls, until I realized a great truth.

The lessons taught by the great masters also lead to vast success in the material world. They were fully aware of this. But they never spoke about it, because they were more concerned about spiritual growth.

So, am I saying that deliberately pursuing a spiritual path is the way to material gain?

Yes, Virginia, that is *exactly* what I am saying. You *can* have your cake and eat it too!

There is a catch, and it took me decades to truly understand this. You cannot set foot on the spiritual path expecting material success. That will come, but it will arrive as a by-product. It is a consequence. If you try to make it a direct goal, it will disappear.

This is the paradox. It *will* come. But if you start on the path expecting it to come, it will not.

We rush about our lives desperately trying to fill the holes in our psyche with the stuff we acquire, through our striving.

We rush about our lives desperately trying to fill the holes in our psyche with the stuff we acquire, through our striving. We become hungry ghosts, devouring what comes in our path. Our peace of mind and ability to experience tranquil joy are the first casualties.

Most of us ignore the solution that has been provided to us by sages throughout the ages—a solution that provides both abundance and spiritual growth.

Did you see *The Karate Kid*? Daniel is beaten up by goons and asks Mr Miyagi to teach him karate so he can protect himself. He is also looking for revenge. Mr Miyagi sets him sanding floors, waxing his car and painting his house. Frustrated and angry, Daniel accuses Mr Miyagi of using him as a servant. He almost stalks off. Mr Miyagi asks him to look in his eyes and then attacks him.

Taken by surprise, Daniel instinctively and skilfully defends himself. That is when he learns that waxing, sanding and painting have given him the muscle memory for karate blocks and punches.

It's pretty much the same story with the teachings from the world's wisdom traditions.

You are born. You will die. Use the little time you have to break free from the great illusion in which you are ensnared.

But the steps you take to do this will also benefit you *within* the illusion.

Stand back and let that happen organically, and on its own. Your focus will be on personal growth.

Are you driven to accomplish? Learn how to avoid the struggle.

You don't have to make trade-offs. Both joy and success can be your lot in life.

56

KEEP STRUGGLING? OR THROW IN THE TOWEL?

Aphorisms and proverbs sometimes pack powerful wisdom. We are fond of quoting them and using them to guide our behaviour or explain it. But have you noticed how many of them contradict one another?

We should 'look before we leap', but unfortunately 'he who hesitates is lost'.

'Many hands make light work', but, alas, 'too many cooks spoil the broth'.

'Wise men think alike', but 'fools seldom differ'.

'Absence makes the heart grow fonder' unless, of course, you are 'out of sight, out of mind'.

'The pen is mightier than the sword', except in the land where 'actions speak louder than words'.

That brings me to a dilemma we all face, sooner or later. We are stuck in a situation that is suffocating and sucks the energy out of us as thoroughly as an efficient Dementor. Perhaps, it is a job we hate though we have tried our level best to learn and stay motivated.

Perhaps, it is a marriage in which we are stifled. We try

to be sensitive to our partner's needs, but we are miserable and unfulfilled.

Maybe we have started a business and it is going nowhere in a hurry, and we have tried everything we know and are running out of funds to keep the lights on.

Do we keep at it with all the vigour we can muster with our dispirited soul, because victory comes to those who persist and never give up? Or do we conserve our energy and quit the battlefield so we can live to fight another day?

Everyone who has taken my Creativity and Personal Mastery course has grappled with their version of this dilemma. Many have asked me for help and advice.

We have been told over and over again that persistence is a virtue. There are tales galore of how someone was struck with all manner of adversity but hung in determinedly, and eventually achieved great success.

In my programme, I have a module where I show participants that an 'intolerable' situation is so largely because we have defined it in that manner and reinforced this label with our mental chatter and models. Many have reported that, with a change in thinking, a toxic situation became bearable, even enjoyable.

Many have reported that, with a change in thinking, a toxic situation became bearable, even enjoyable.

Another module points out that one of the ways the universe signals to us that it is time to make a change is by making us miserable where we are.

So, where does this leave you? What should you do in your particular position?

Here is a framework to use in such situations.

When we are confronted with a dilemma or a decision fork, most of us tend to ask: 'What should I do?' We desperately try to think of the pros and cons of each possible course of action, and somehow balance and evaluate and compare them in a convoluted manner.

Ask this question instead: 'Who am I being?'

Take the following example. If you believe you are stuck in a toxic job environment, then you are being a victim of external circumstances and indulging in self-pity. You are also being me-centered and are definitely not in an emotional domain of appreciation and gratitude.

Is this where you want to be?

Assuredly not.

Who do you want to be? You want to be a person who is calm and serene, grateful for the many things in their life and willing to work hard to 'improve' the areas where your preferences are not being met.

Think about who you want to be, and then pour your emotional energy into that being. In other words, *be* the person you want to be.

This takes a bit of practice, but it is not as hard as you may think. Initially, there will be a feeling that you are kidding yourself or playing a game, but this will pass. You will actually be able to, at least for the time being, become who you want to be.

Now, ask yourself what this person would do in your situation. And the answer will pop out easily.

You may decide to remain and try harder. You may decide to quit and go elsewhere.

It does not matter, because here is a great truth for you to ponder: Who you are being is *much* more important than what you are doing.

57

THIS ILLUSION IS WRECKING YOUR LIFE!

There is an illusion you hold on to, even though your own experience shows that it is just that—an illusion. You know it, but you behave as if this myth were true. Much suffering results from this. You believe it. Oh, how you believe it! But it is false, and you know it!

What is this delusion that holds you in thrall?

It is the notion that you are one, single, permanent self that is present all the time.

I *know* this is not true.

The resolute me that greets the morning with joy and determines to eat healthfully and exercise is not the same person who, having had a good dinner and brushed his teeth, decides the perfect way to end the day is with a deep-fried, salty snack.

The good-natured me, who fully believes that the universe gives hints, is not the snarling brute who emerges when he has sunk into a comfortable armchair to watch his favourite TV show and the universe, through his lovely wife, reminds him that he promised to do the laundry.

The protagonist of the bestseller *Sybil* had 16 separate personalities. You may not be a pathological case, but I bet you have more.

I certainly do.

Perhaps, you can relate to this entertaining piece written by Obi Ejimofo, who took my Creativity and Personal Mastery course at London Business School.

> My Nigerian me was caught on camera last Monday battling with the UK-born me for control of the kitchen. Spontaneous me sneaked in between the two and whipped up a spicy stir-fry with ingredients from both warring camps.
>
> Mindless me grabbed the steamy plate, leapt on the couch, opened up my laptop, turned the TV volume down a notch and began to make a phone call while furiously blowing on the meal to cool it down.
>
> CPM [Creativity and Personal Mastery] me wagged a stern finger and negotiated a more mindful experience of the meal (the TV stayed on as a compromise).
>
> Worry me applauded the choice of fish over red meat and the variety of vegetables but worried about the liberal amounts of groundnut oil used.
>
> Indulgent me tucked in, cleaned the plate, went for another helping and topped it all off with three glasses of wine.
>
> Sporty me bemoaned my foot injury, no football for a few weeks. Music me couldn't decide whether to play Cuban jazz or neo-soul, while CPM me denounced all the other me's as mere manifestations of mind chatter.
>
> Nigerian me was sulking, UK me flicked through the Dutch channels for something in English, while Don Juan me wondered yet again whether the ladies at the spinning class giggled for Sporty me or Black me.
>
> Black me chuckled to himself—he felt he knew the answer…

Creative me fretted and tugged and squirmed; he wanted to write and draw and make music again. 'Damn this MBA,' Creative me said.

MBA me fretted and tugged and squirmed. He missed the classes, the debate, the broadening of the mind.

Worry me sniffed, remembering that I turn thirty-four in less than a month. Nigerian me concurred; my mum wants to see that me married. Family me agreed; he wanted kids. Career-minded me joined the thought. I should have been far more successful by now. UK-born me just wanted to be back in London.

CPM me joined forces with Sporty me and Creative me, morphed into Positive me, bribed Mindless me to stay out of it, and kicked Anxiety me to the curb.

Music me decided on some Cuban jazz...

All of me stretched, lay back and relaxed to enjoy the vibes...except for Worry me. 'Who was going to do the washing up?'

Do you recognize yourself? You have many selves. Some of these selves behave in ways that greatly upset other selves. That is just the way it is. Problems arise because you think there is only one permanent self, and this self is accountable for all your sins of omission and commission.

You have many selves. Some of these selves behave in ways that greatly upset other selves. That is just the way it is.

Recognize that these selves come and go. They are all equally unreal.

You are beyond that. You are none of these selves but rather the observer of these selves. Rest in that state.

58

MENTAL CHATTER IS FAKE NEWS!

'Fool me once, shame on you. Fool me twice, shame on me.' I am not sure whether that expression originated as a nursery rhyme or a random bit of doggerel, but it rings true. If you are like most people I know, you certainly believe that you are smart and it is very difficult to deceive you—and if a person does succeed in hoodwinking you, then that is the last time they will be able to do so.

You will not trust that person again and will double- and triple-verify everything they tell you. Now, let's consider Paul.

> Paul was depressed. He was one of two executive vice presidents (VP) at his company and had just launched a major marketing initiative that had already increased revenues by 20 per cent, and would probably double them in less than six months.
>
> He should have been a shoo-in for CEO. Ralph, the current CEO, was planning on retiring by the end of the year, but a heart attack had hastened the timetable.
>
> The board was meeting right now to formalize it, and Paul had not been invited. He had expected to be called to explain the initiative he had launched, but he hadn't even

been notified of the meeting, let alone asked to speak.

Paul knew that Ralph favoured Steve, the other executive VP. The two lunched together regularly and were often seen laughing and confabulating.

Steve had asked for an investigation into whether Paul's initiative was a good 'fit' with the brand profile of the product, and wondered aloud if the increased sales were actually a sign of 'stockpiling' and would lead to decreased sales in the future.

'****ing SOB,' Paul muttered viciously, 'sucking up because he just can't get ahead any other way.' He conveniently forgot that he also had tried to set up regular lunch meetings with Ralph, but was rebuffed.

The phone buzzed.

It was Ralph asking him if he could come to the boardroom right away. He said it was important.

As he passed Steve's office, Paul took a quick peek in. Steve had a stand-up desk, and his laptop was connected to a wall monitor. It was displaying the agenda for today's meeting—the one Paul had not been invited to and not even informed about—and the first item was 'CEO succession'.

That's it, he thought bitterly. *The weasel has bad-mouthed me, and he won. Darn if I will remain with the company.*

He decided he would resign right away. No point in putting on a brave front. He would find a CEO position elsewhere or, failing that, would simply retire. He did not want his career to end this way, but that was the way the cookie crumbled.

Much to his surprise, everybody burst into cheers when he entered and there was a lot of clapping.

'What—what…?' he stammered.

'I was going to announce it next month,' said Ralph jovially, 'but I have to go to the hospital again, and they want me to stay for an indefinite period. So, I thought I'd do it right away.'

'Do what?' asked Paul, puzzled.

'Announce you as the new CEO,' said Ralph. 'It was always between you and Steve. Steve just presented the findings of the study he commissioned about your new marketing drive, and it was roses all the way. He would be delighted to work with you as you settle into your role but will be leaving in a few months.'

It turned out that Steve was about to become Ralph's son-in-law, and was starting his own company with his fiancée and with Ralph's blessing.

A smile broke out on Paul's face.

It was a good day after all.

We are all Paul.

Have you ever fretted because you did not receive a phone call intimating safe arrival from your children driving home late at night?

Have you watched the talking heads on news channels talking about soaring crime, and become concerned about what is happening to society and the world in general?

All of this has its root in a simple phenomenon.

Mental chatter.

Mental chatter is that internal monologue you have going on in your head—*all* the time.

Paul wondered if he would become CEO and engaged with this fleeting thought, and his mental chatter created an elaborate scenario where Steve was busy plotting to derail him and Ralph was a willing accomplice.

The pundits spin a tale based on today's fragmentary evidence, and you promptly pile on with your own stories about where the world is headed, and feel dejected and even depressed.

When I was head of consumer research at Data Resources, I wrote a report on how the personal computer and Artificial Intelligence would change the world. My brilliant prediction was that so much grunt work would be done by computers that we would have oodles of leisure, and I even speculated on the 30-hour work week becoming the norm.

Mental chatter is fake news.

We engage too much with our thoughts and spin tales that we believe. And no matter how many times our mental chatter has demonstrably led us astray, we believe it every time it tells us something. So, to improve your life, remember this: *Mental chatter is fake news.*

Do not believe it. Be aware of it and double- and triple-check everything it tells you. Do not let it determine your mood or the emotional domain you occupy.

I received dozens of comments—mostly laudatory—when I first wrote about how mental chatter is fake news.

One of my former students wrote:

> Great article, Professor, and I agree with the general premise, but I always struggle between leveraging the mental chatter to build a preemptive defence mechanism versus the fake news aspect that leads to constant stress. If we stop listening to mental chatter completely, we will always end up being reactive and that might also lead to potential problems. Nature might have given us, as humans, mental chatter to take care of things before disaster strikes. If we completely stop listening to mental chatter, we also

> stop being strategic and slacken on planning. On the other hand, the constant 'fake news' in the head is very stressful—I agree. How do we balance between the two?

His point here is that sometimes our mental chatter might—just might—be indicating that there is something going on to which we should pay attention.

And he is right!

But he is right at level one. And I will tell you what you can do at this level.

On this level, you are going around doing your thing and there is this thing called mental chatter that grabs you by the throat and drags you to places you don't want to go. It creates all kinds of problems in your life, and much of the time it inflames and incites you with information that is flat-out false.

On this level, you watch your mental chatter and become an observer. This creates distance between you and your mental chatter. Your mental chatter then can no longer take you to dark places. Remember, mental chatter just is. It is neither 'good' nor 'bad'. Your problems arise because you identify with your mental chatter and become your mental chatter.

So, in response to my student's query, the answer is simple. Not necessarily easy, but simple.

Remain a witness, and do not let your emotions take over. Examine what your mental chatter tells you and take it under advisement. It is simply a notification, like the warning light that comes on in your car when you run low on gas.

If you treat your mental chatter in this way, and studiously avoid believing it and getting emotionally wrought by its message, you are just fine.

As I said, it is not easy but it can be done. You just need to practise it diligently.

Level two is where it gets really interesting, and what I say now may not make sense to you. If this is the case, just ignore the rest of this section.

There is a duality in level one. There is you, and you are also the observer of this mental chatter that is going on.

But this separate existence of you is itself fake news!

What you consider as 'me' and are immersed in is a body–mind–intellect that is fictitious. It arises from thought and is insubstantial. It is like a dream.

You are *not* the body–mind–intellect complex. You are pure awareness contemplating it. That is what you have always been, and that is beyond space and time.

The Indian sage, Ramana Maharshi, would frequently direct questions put to him back to this level.

A visitor would ask him what to do because he was anxious/fearful/sad, and the sage would ask him to contemplate who is anxious/fearful/sad.

This is the most direct path to enlightenment, realization, moksha or whatever you choose to call it.

And it is really the only thing that matters.

One of the most empowering things you can do when faced with circumstances that are beyond your control is to shift the way you look at the situation. This is not to say that you overlook or minimize your concerns—your emotions are what they are. However, you can reduce or alleviate any suffering you may be experiencing as a result of fear by turning within and becoming the observer of your reactions and emotions.

The powerful tools and insights in this book can aid you in managing stress, creating peace, navigating challenges and transmuting unease during these uncertain times.

Be an observer of fear—and remember, you are connected to everything.

59

YOU CAN'T SOLVE AN INTERNAL PROBLEM WITH EXTERNAL ACTION

Yet, this is what you try to do again and again!

I have taught Creativity and Personal Mastery at many top business schools, including Columbia, Kellogg, London Business School and Berkeley. And without fail, the same incident happens. Sometimes it happens more than once. A woman—sometimes a man—tells me about a trip she took to some remote part of the world. And she tells me about the people and her experience.

'They had *nothing*,' she says feelingly. 'But they seemed so happy.'

And there is more than a note of wistfulness in her voice. There is a sense of unfairness. How could they have nothing and be so joyful, while she had everything and can hardly wait for the 'sleep that knits up the ravell'd sleeve of care'*?

This reminds me of a *60 Minutes* segment on Darfur, at the height of the refugee crisis. If ever there was a deprived population, it was the inhabitants of Darfur at that time.

*'The Tragedy of Macbeth', *Shakespeare.mit*, https://tinyurl.com/2p8rmhmd. Accessed on 11 August 2023.

And in that hellhole, there were kids who trailed the CBS correspondents and peered into the cameras with wonder. And, at that instant, there was unquestionably genuine, unadulterated happiness radiating from them.

At that instant, there was unquestionably genuine, unadulterated happiness radiating from them.

The people my student referenced, the children of Darfur, did not have hot and cold running water, reliable power, indoor toilets or air conditioning. They certainly did not have smartphones, the Internet or email.

But they did have the ability to make peace with their circumstances.

Kurt Vonnegut supposedly was with Joseph Heller at a party given by a billionaire on Shelter Island. He nudged Heller, and told him that their host made more in a single day than the cumulative sales of *Catch-22* in its entire publishing history.

Unimpressed, Heller responded, 'Yes, but I have something he will never have—enough.'[*]

And there you have the dilemma of our society of strivers—we have a gaping hole in our being, a sense that we are somehow incomplete, that we need something to make us whole. We try to patch ourselves up with attainment, accomplishment and acquisitions. We try to become famous and wealthy and powerful and accomplished.

But the hole remains. It may even grow larger.

So, here is a thought for you: You cannot solve an internal problem with external action.

---

[*] Carlson, Ben, 'Enough.', *A Wealth of Common Sense*, 23 December 2013, https://tinyurl.com/yckhyy24. Accessed on 11 August 2023.

60

WHAT DOES IT MEAN TO WORK WITH LOVE?

Sometimes the lesson you need to learn is right at home, but you have spent a lifetime avoiding it—and you suffer totally unnecessary misery as a result.

To give you some background, I do not like gardening. I do like reading in my wife's gorgeous gardens with colourful flowers and butterflies flitting to-and-fro, but they do not make my heart soar. And I emphatically do not like planting, weeding, watering, fertilizing and all the chores you have to do to create a beautiful garden.

My wife, on the other hand, loves gardening, which is fine by me. But what I do not appreciate is the way she tries to rope me in to help her in the misguided hope that I will also start to like it.

She had to go away for three days and strictly enjoined me to water the plants she had grown in pots. The automatic sprinklers took care of the rest of the flora. The temperature soared into the 90s on all three days, and I completely forgot my promise on the first day. I tried to make it up by double-dousing them in water for the next two days.

When my wife returned, she was really upset and laced into me.

'You just poured water on them,' she accused.

I thought that was exactly what I was supposed to do, and said so.

'No, no, no!' she protested. She was almost in tears. 'The flowers are delicate. Look how many you killed by subjecting them to a heavy stream of water.'

She explained further: The plants were babies and needed to be watered with love, with a gentle trickle to the roots and not a barrage from the top.

I observed her, and that is exactly what she did. The love with which she pruned, watered and weeded was evident. I had just never noticed it before.

She was correct. There was no love in my action. I poured water on the pots with resentment at what I considered a chore. There were other things I would rather have been doing. Until she pointed it out with some vigour, I did not even notice that I was harming the life forms that I was supposed to be nurturing.

I remembered the poem 'On Work' by Kahlil Gibran that had impressed me so much that I put it in the syllabus for my programme:

> And all work is empty save when there is love;
>
> And when you work with love you bind yourself to yourself, and to one another, and to God.
>
> And what is it to work with love?
>
> It is to weave the cloth with threads drawn from your heart, even as if your beloved were to wear that cloth.
>
> It is to build a house with affection, even as if your beloved were to dwell in that house.
>
> It is to sow seeds with tenderness and reap the harvest with joy, even as if your beloved were to eat the fruit.
>
> It is to charge all things you fashion with a breath of

> your own spirit,
>
> And to know that all the blessed dead are standing about you and watching.
>
> Often have I heard you say, as if speaking in sleep, 'He who works in marble, and finds the shape of his own soul in the stone, is nobler than he who ploughs the soil. And he who seizes the rainbow to lay it on a cloth in the likeness of man, is more than he who makes the sandals for our feet.'
>
> But I say, not in sleep but in the over-wakefulness of noontide, that the wind speaks not more sweetly to the giant oaks than to the least of all the blades of grass;
>
> And he alone is great who turns the voice of the wind into a song made sweeter by his own loving.
>
> Work is love made visible.*

We race around desperately seeking work that we love, and a career we can be passionate about. And we totally forget to put love into what we are doing as we seek these pastures that we think are greener.

We totally forget to put love into what we are doing as we seek these pastures that we think are greener.

It is perfectly all right to seek betterment—in finances, in career prospects, in greater satisfaction. But do so while you are pouring love into what you are doing now.

Putting love into what you do is better than searching for what you love.

Who knows, if you do this sincerely, you may find that your perfect station is right where you are now.

So, I will endeavour to water with care and feeling. Even with love.

---

*Gibran, Kahlil, *The Prophet,* Knopf Doubleday Publishing Group, 1952.

61

WHO ARE YOU BEING?

We wake up every morning and go to work. Or to whatever we do. And each day we have a choice.

We can break rocks. Or we can help build a cathedral.

I cannot define for you the cathedral you can build, or are building. Only you can do that. But I can tell you that, unless you define that cathedral you will eke out a mediocre existence punctuated with flashes of pleasure.

We can break rocks. Or we can help build a cathedral.

That's just the way it is. The following is one of many stories I could tell you that demonstrate this principle.

It was an exclusive girl's school, and three newly admitted girls felt somewhat ill at ease when they arrived. Possibly, it was this sense of being out of place that drew them together, or perhaps it was a recognition that they shared exceptional intelligence; or the fact that they were the only ones who were not already friends with someone else.

Whatever it was, they clustered together and became best friends.

After graduation they scattered to their respective countries, but they kept in touch. In those days, it was not common for women to leave the house and almost unheard of for them to work. Teaching was quasi-respectable, and all three became kindergarten teachers.

Once in a great while they would somehow arrange to be in the same place at the same time. There was joy in these meetings, and much reminiscing. There was also an undercurrent of sorrow and longing as they realized that life was not unfolding in the way they thought it would, for any of them. Each coped with this in her own way.

Mary saw herself as the temporary custodian of the children of wealthy, uncaring parents and resented having to wipe their noses; help them pull on galoshes; or having to make sure they ate their lunch and snacks. The children sensed her dislike and resisted learning. They did poorly on tests and her principal spoke to her about lack of performance, and this infuriated her even more.

She was bitter when she retired and went to her grave soon after. Not a single student or parent attended her funeral.

Joan saw herself as teaching reading, 'riting and 'rithmetic to young children and keeping order. Some of her kids were bright and some were dullards, and she did what she could with each. She was a trifle sorry to retire but not altogether unhappy because she could no longer keep up with the unlimited energy of her young charges.

When she passed on, some of her one-time students, who lived close by, came to say goodbye and one of them delivered a fine eulogy. They then went about their business.

Early on, Eleanor, like Mary, disliked what she felt she was being forced to do. Then she saw what her attitude was doing to her. She was resentful each day, snapped querulously at her own daughter and was withdrawn from her husband. And she was tired, always tired.

She determined to love each child who was entrusted to her. They were the clay, and she was the potter—and each of her pots would be a work of art.

She saw that they were enthralled by stories, and she told them tales of great heroes and how they overcame insurmountable odds and accomplished incredible feats of service. She encouraged them to dream great dreams, and also to start laying foundations for the castles they built in the air.

Her eyes twinkled and her steps were light. When she reached mandatory retirement age, the school board voted twice to give her an extension and then simply made her the honorary chairperson of a committee they created specially to give her a legitimate reason to keep coming back.

When she passed on, people came from all over the country to bid her adieu. The prime minister made a special visit because he was one of her former students, and remembered that his first desire to enter public service arose when she challenged him to set right something he was complaining about. There were newspaper editorials, mourning on blogs and a Twitter-facilitated minute of silence that thousands observed.

And many a mother wished her son would have a teacher like Eleanor.

Here is my question to you: When you go to work tomorrow, will you be like Mary? Or Joan? Or will you decide to do what it takes to be Eleanor?

Remember—it matters what you do. It matters *much* more who you are being as you do it!

62

YOU ARE NOT GOING ANYWHERE!

Acknowledging such might be your path to liberation.

As a public speaker, I have frequently illustrated our tendency to remain frantically busy while getting nowhere through the example of a hamster on a wheel.

Virtually everybody can relate to the example.

In fact, 'hamster on a wheel' has become the shorthand for a meaningless life filled with unfulfilling action.

An alumnus of my programme challenged me. 'Professor Rao, the hamster isn't trying to go somewhere. He is simply exercising and having a fun time.'

There is a lesson here for you and me and everyone else.

We are going to die someday. It could be tomorrow, next week or decades from now.

For whatever reason—karma, destiny, happenstance—we are in our present predicament. We frequently feel that we are spinning helplessly because we want to get somewhere but are unable to. That is when a sense of futility arises.

Turn it around. Do the activity to the best of your ability, but give up the attachment to any particular outcome. The result you want may appear. Or it may not. Focus on enjoying the activity, and doing it to the best of your ability.

Your life will improve. You will be a hamster on the wheel that is having a rip-roaring time.

I bet you made resolutions for this year, and I further bet that many of you have already seen some of these fall by the wayside!

Let me share something with you that really works.

It is probably accurate to say that virtually everything we do is a part of our quest to be happy. We want work we enjoy, that pays us well. We want loving friends and family. We seek stimulation and diverse experiences because these are all things that make us happy. Or at least we think they will do so.

We also believe that 'more' will make us happier, and we are on a relentless quest for this. More money, a bigger house, a larger or more luxurious car, a more beautiful partner, more power, greater prominence, higher position and on and on. Some of us go beyond material stuff and venture into experience. We need to go to more exotic and far-flung places on vacation or experience uncommon thrills, from helicopter skiing in remote snowy wildernesses to rare liquors and liqueurs from esoteric fruits.

And we do get a rush of pleasure, but then we come back to where we were and begin the fruitless quest again.

We are goal-driven creatures, each of us, and we strive with the notion that if we reach that goal we will be happier.

This is the if–then trap of life, and nobody warns us of its danger. In fact, many of those who wish us well and whom we hold dear are ignorant of the snare and actively egg us on. We are urged to 'go for it', told that we can do it and encouraged to not stop until we reach the goal.

The if–then trap gets us to lurch drunkenly from one activity to another, to accomplish something or acquire something more so we can be happy.

This is a model of life, and it is a flawed model. It is simply not true. At some level we recognize this, but it is an intellectual understanding and not very deep. So, each time we acquire something or accomplish a cherished goal and the initial thrill wears away, we set our sights on something else and begin the chase again. In other words, we tinker with what we put on the 'if' side of the if–then model but never realize it is the model itself that is faulty and that changing what we put on one side makes no real difference.

As we go through life, we quickly discover that actions are within our control but the outcome is not. Random events casually derail our carefully laid plans. We have an important meeting in a different city and go to the airport well in time to make our flight, only to find it cancelled because of mechanical problems. We work diligently and are loyal to our boss, but he is shunted aside by an ambitious rival and our career is in the doldrums.

Much of the time we do not get the outcome we want, and some of the time we get an outcome diametrically opposed to our desire. So, if we are fixated on the outcome we are setting ourselves up for angst and depression.

There is a way out, and that is to invest in the process and not the outcome. John Wooden, the first person to reach the Basketball Hall of Fame as both a player and a coach, expressed it well:

> Many people are surprised to learn that in twenty-seven years at UCLA, I never once talked about winning. Instead, I would tell my players before the games, 'When it's over, I want your head up. And there's only one way for your head to be up, and that's for you to know, not me, that you gave the best effort of which you are capable.

> If you do that, then the score really doesn't matter, although I have a feeling that if you do that, the score will be to your liking.' I honestly, deeply believe that in not stressing winning as such, we won more than we would have if we had stressed outscoring opponents.*

We still do exactly what we have always done: we set goals. But once we have done so, we no longer obsess about it. We simply pour all our attention and energy into doing what we have determined we must do to achieve that goal. We do not fret. We do not spend sleepless nights tossing and turning. We work diligently on doing what we must.

When we work in this manner, we discover something strange and unexpected—we experience the work we do as a true blessing. Tarthang Tulku expressed this beautifully:

> Caring about our work, liking it, even loving it, seems strange when we see work only as a way to make a living. But when we see work as a way to deepen and enrich all of our experience, each one of us can find this caring within our hearts, and awaken it in those around us, using every aspect of our work to learn and grow. . . . Every kind of work can be a pleasure. Even simple household tasks can be an opportunity to exercise and expand our caring, our effectiveness, our responsiveness. As we respond with caring and vision to all work, we develop our capacity to respond fully to all of life. Every action generates positive energy which can be shared with others. These qualities of caring and responsiveness are the greatest gift we can offer.**

---

*Toski, Bob, Davis Love Jr and Robert Carney, *How to Feel a Real Golf Swing: Mind-Body Techniques from Two of Golf's Greatest Teachers,* Crown, 1998.

**Tulku, Tarthang, *Skillful Means: Patterns for Success,* Dharma Pub., 1991.

When we approach what we do in this manner, we find that our emotional well-being is not affected by whether we achieve our goal. Paradoxically, as Wooden points out, this enlightened detachment makes it far more likely that we will actually achieve the goal we are striving for.

In the manifesto for my programme, I state that you should enrol if you wish to discover meaning in your life. Many participants come to the Creativity and Personal Mastery course because they see I am passionate about what I do, and they want to discover similar passion in their lives.

I paint a vivid picture in the manifesto of how you can wake up every morning brimming with good cheer, and vibrantly alive. Of how your life can be full of meaning and purpose, and how enrolling in my programme is a good first step toward getting there.

This does end up being true. Countless individuals find that the spark comes back into their lives after they take my programme.

Today, I would like to go deeper and say that the very quest for meaning is fruitless.

There is a belief that I can 'find' something or adopt an attitude or perspective that energizes me, and makes me happy. This is a false belief. And even the notion that there is an 'I' that needs to be happy and fulfilled is a delusion.

We bring our grasping, acquisitive minds to this quest and each time we reiterate our desire to find meaning, we implant in our mind that we are currently leading a meaningless life. I have been doing this for decades. So have you.

Life *is*. It has always been and will always be. This existence itself is the meaning.

You *do not* discover meaning. It discovers you. You help it discover you by creating it. As long as you *do* something to *get* or *be* something else, you are trapped in the spider web of delusion, and sucked deeper into the illusion of despair.

Thus, if you meditate to calm your mind and relieve tension, you are stuck. If you meditate because you would like to be enlightened, you are stuck. The *only* way out is to meditate because you meditate. Remember: *The purpose of washing dishes is not to get them clean. The purpose of washing dishes is to wash the dishes.*

The purpose of washing dishes is not to get them clean. The purpose of washing dishes is to wash the dishes.

If you find this dense and difficult to get your arms around, I don't blame you. After many decades, I am just beginning to understand it myself. But do play around with this idea as you would roll an oversized bit of candy in your mouth. The candy will dissolve and become pleasurable.

And you will understand what I have just shared.

And perhaps, meaning will discover you.

QUESTIONS AND EXERCISES TO ACCELERATE YOUR TRANSFORMATION

The following questions and exercises will help you incorporate the concepts in this book into your life. Try the exercises after reading the chapters, or anytime you want a quick refresher course on the principles and strategies that the book offers.

Chapters 1–2

1. Recall as many instances as you can when you changed your mind about someone or some event based on the information you received. For example, you thought your elderly neighbour was brushing you off by not returning your phone call, and then you discovered that his daughter accidentally deleted his voicemail before he listened to the messages.
2. Think deeply about your values, beliefs and behaviour patterns. Identify and articulate, as clearly as you can, three to five mental models that you hold and according to which you act. *It is important that all these models be of great significance to you.* You should have at least one model in each of these categories: (i) your job or professional development (e.g., how to get a good job), (ii) your personal life (e.g., how to raise children) and (iii) a broad and all-encompassing model (i.e., a 'this is the way the world works' model).
3. Take a break for a couple of weeks, and then come back to the

models you have outlined and study them carefully. Are they serving you well? Would your experience of life be better if you tweaked some of these models or even replaced them entirely? Try making the changes you identify. Do not work on more than one model at a time.

Chapters 3–6

1. What is your definition of freedom and how does it compare to notions of freedom presented within these pages?
2. How does fear become a cage for you, and what role does your own mental chatter have in creating that cage? What role do others have in it, or perhaps your occupation?
3. Procure a journal for the purpose of writing down, at any given moment, when you feel like you are 'in the cage'. Describe the circumstances causing the caged sensation, whether it be from within your mental model; a product of your mental chatter; caused by others that you are allowing to influence you; or by your work occupation. When you have collected 10 scenarios, examine your notes to see what they have in common. If you know your enemy, you can better fight him off!
4. Now pick one of the scenarios, and dismantle the cage. For example, a physician was very interested in taking my course but could not because one of the meeting slots coincided with days when he was on call. We had a long conversation during which I shared the notion that, many times, barriers exist only between our ears. He promptly registered for the course and informed his partners that one of them would need to cover for him on that weekend. He did not ask for permission or discuss the matter. He simply told them matter-of-factly, and they accommodated him. Once you get the hang of this, do something similar for all the other scenarios you have identified. Some will be easy. Some will feel insurmountable.

Don't give up on the latter. Come back to them in a few months, and then again after some more months. You will be surprised at how soon the fences and barriers break down.

Chapters 7–10

1. How do your expectations and perspective potentially get in the way of your happiness?
2. When you criticize those around you, are you in some way projecting what you don't like about yourself? Are they the problem, or is it you?
3. Choose three things you tend to complain about and write them down on separate pages. Perhaps it is your job, your spouse or even your children's lack of respect or success. Create a list of five positive attributes to the very things (or people) that you tend to discount as unpleasant, tedious, unsavoury or not worth your time. Focus only on these positive attributes, and note if there is a change in your attitude toward the things or people you disliked.
4. Passion does not exist in your job. It exists inside you. Pick something in your job that you find boring or dispiriting. Can you change your perspective so that it becomes something you are passionate about? Or, at least, enthusiastic about? One of my students was tasked with organizing meetings and taking minutes at those meetings. She hated it. And then she saw that she could help shape the agenda at the meetings, and ensure that her priorities got airtime. Her distaste changed to liking.

Chapters 11–13

1. What keeps you awake at night? Be honest and specific as you consider the ways your mental chatter keeps you from achieving peace and satisfaction.
2. How often do you conscientiously feel gratitude for the good

in your life? How about the good in *yourself*?

3. Think of your awareness as a flashlight. A flashlight illuminates anything you shine it on. Consciously, deliberately, shine it on the good things in your life and keep it there. For example, you go to an expensive restaurant with your partner to celebrate your anniversary, and the waitress messes up your order. You can get annoyed at this mishap, and ruin the occasion. Or you can be grateful for an intimate evening and perhaps, even for the opportunity to sample a dish you would never have ordered.

Chapters 14–17

1. Do you have an addiction? An unhealthy habit that may even be so subtle, coming in small doses, that you do not recognize how it interferes with your success or happiness? List all that you identify.
2. How do you fuel your habit? Perhaps you indulge your habit because it is easy. Or comfortable. Like eating junk food rather than assembling a healthy salad. This is also 'feeding the wolf'. Does feeding the wolf make you feel better about yourself for a short while but worse on the whole? What can you do to think differently?
3. Think about something you do that is unhealthy. This may well be an addiction you identified in the first exercise above. It may be smoking or drinking, or too-frequent dessert indulgence. It may be a codependent relationship that is negative and damaging, but also addictive. Perhaps you gamble, either in a casino or online. Or you comfort yourself with shopping, spending money you may not have. Maybe you drown your anxiety by being consistently negative, and thereby keeping your expectations low. Whatever your vice is, it is probably something that you have outgrown (or would in all honesty like to) but that you, for whatever reason, have

allowed to linger. List the excuses you make to continue leaning on it, then cross them out. Come up with a plan to remove it from your life. Do research and devote time to this endeavour.

Chapters 18–24

1. What in your life has given you the greatest fulfilment? When did you feel good about yourself that had nothing to do with others applauding you or rewarding you or external validation of any kind? What can you do to bring this feeling back into your life?
2. Every time you are angry, overwhelmed, sad, fearful, driven by lust or anxious, your breathing is fast and shallow. The next time you find yourself in the grip of a negative emotion, pause! Straighten your spine, and take 10 very deep, very slow breaths. See how you feel after you have done this. Then go back to what you were doing.
3. Treat every mishap that happens to you as if it were a person. Speak to that person. Let the person know that you will not allow them to determine how your day goes. Say, you are driving to an important meeting and get a flat tire on the highway. It takes an hour for the tow truck to come, and longer for the service station to fix your tire. Let your punctured tire know that you will not let it ruin your perfect day. Mean this. Then, set about rescheduling your meeting and doing what you need to do from a space of tranquil ease.

Chapters 25–30

1. Have there been any events in your life that you classified as terrible disasters that you now recognize as not so bad? Perhaps even good? Pick something that you are grappling with in your life right now—something that you think is a problem or bad

thing. Can you visualize any scenario by which, in a few years, that thing could turn out to be wonderful? Then, ask a further question: What can I do now to bring about this wonderful result?

2. Watch yourself when you have conversations—with your boss, your partner, your children, your clients. Do you pay attention to what they are saying? Do you note changes in tone and demeanour that indicate emotional undertones? Or are you wrapped up in formulating your next comment? Try to have an entire conversation without ever using the words 'I', 'me' or 'my'. See how difficult this is.
3. Much of the sorrow in our lives comes from our resistance to what is. In small ways, try to let go of your preferences and enjoy what life puts in your way. You may want to sit down and watch your favourite TV show, but your wife wants to go out for dinner. Go, and determine to have a good time. Make a note of how often you do this, and try to increase the number of such occasions. Note how this affects your experience of life.

Chapters 31–36

1. Are you taking steps, each and every morning, to ensure that you are about to have a fantastic day? What ambitions or misconceptions about needing to be unique may be getting in the way of actually enjoying your life? What role does your past, and not being able to let go of it, have in your discontent?
2. Do you make an effort to step outside yourself? How could you push yourself to do so even more?
3. Set aside a time each evening, for two to three weeks in a row, when you reflect on whether it was a fantastic day or not. Journal about it, and set an alarm reminder so that you do not miss a day. The effort will make you more aware of how you can shape yourself toward greater satisfaction.

Chapters 37–43

1. What is the difference between striving for its own sake and striving for a purpose? In what ways do you merely strive toward a goal or rigid expectation, focussed only on the outcome, and in what other ways do you strive for a purpose? Create lists to help you make visual distinctions between the two. How can you make your life more effortless or joyful by refocussing around the second list?
2. Are you making your choices and setting goals deliberately, with positive results in mind, while letting the universe guide you? When you fail to meet a goal, do you pause to rethink the purpose, or do you just work harder without reflecting?
3. How does the way you view other people get in the way of letting go and following your path, while allowing a greater wisdom to guide you? Consider the person in your life who is giving you the most trouble. It might be your spouse, or it might be your boss. Write down specific things about this person that bother you. Then, go down your list and truly consider whether it would be easier to let go of attributes you cannot change or to keep struggling against them. Consider how your life would be easier if you accepted them.

Chapters 44–50

1. Everyone has their baggage. This is something we hear all the time. On a sheet of paper, draw a suitcase that nearly fills the page. Inside that suitcase, write down all the people and events from your past that still drag you down. Add the preconceptions and expectations that bring you grief. Draw lines between the people, events and expectations that are connected. Are these people still active in your life today? Have your relationships with them improved? In what ways are they the same? In what ways is it your responsibility, and not theirs,

to make your suitcase lighter?

2. Now, consider what you have given people and what they have given you, physical and otherwise. Do you let go of what may not have felt like a fair exchange? That neighbour who you invited for coffee over and over again, but he never invited you—have you forgiven him? What about those who have hurt you in deeper ways? It may be time to crumple up your suitcase drawing and begin fresh.

Chapters 51–57

1. Go through your wardrobe and pick out articles of clothing that you have not used in two years. Look at each one and ask, 'Do I *really* need you in my life today?' If the answer is no, set it aside. Make a pile of these clothes, and give them away. Now deal with other items in your house—furniture, sheets, bric-a-brac, objets d'art, kitchen stuff, toys, games and so on. Ask of each one, 'Do you bring joy into my life today, right now?' If the answer is no, then give it away.
2. Make your own emotional 'Do I really…?' list. In this list, consider all the emotional baggage, grudges, political biases and so on that you are holding on to. What is it that you really need? How can you refocus your energy on living in the present and helping someone in need, who may not have any of the comforts that you take for granted daily? Spend just one hour researching a local organization that would benefit from a donation of your time. Then approach them and offer your help.
3. Ask yourself frequently, 'Who am I being?' Come up with an extensive list of all the people you are and all the roles you play. Remember, the self is not one permanent entity but ever-changing. Consider which roles you could be more genuine in, and perhaps which ones you could let go of altogether.

Chapters 58–62

1. How is your own mental chatter like fake news? In what ways does your fear of the unknown or concern about others take over, often derailing the peace and tranquility you would otherwise experience in your day?
2. Make a list of the 'anti-mantras' you have created for yourself. Perhaps, it's that you are not ageing gracefully and are worried about how you will age in the future. Perhaps, you keep worrying that your colleague is going to take your promotion or that your son will get hurt while out with his friends late at night. Are these things you have much control over? In what ways can you tackle their nagging persistence in a more organic way, with the intent to eventually let go of all the unknown fears haunting you? Consider your list in the light of internal and external problems, and take an internal approach to making peace with them.
3. Consider all the lists and summaries you have created while moving through this assessment. Flip through the pages and review them. Can you see that the overwhelming majority of the problems that plague you are the result of your mental chatter running amok?
4. Try to imbue all your actions with love. Do this deliberately. When you tip your waiter, wish them and their family well. When someone cuts you off in traffic, send him a blessing rather than a curse. You will forget to do this consistently. Go back to doing it when you remember. How does your experience of life change?

ADVANCED COACHING WITH SRIKUMAR RAO

Roger Federer, Rafael Nadal and Novak Djokovic are all contenders for the title of greatest tennis player who ever lived. Each of them works with a personal coach. Why is this? What is left for them to learn?

In a landmark article in *The New Yorker*, Atul Gawande makes a case for coaching for expert practitioners in all fields. He maintains that coaching, done well, may be the most significant intervention designed for human performance.* Great coaching will make you reach higher orbits of performance and accomplishment.

Great coaching will make you reach higher orbits of performance and accomplishment.

Many entrepreneurs and executives work with coaches. Frequently, these engagements seek to bolster a specific area of executive competence. So, you may work with a coach to improve your listening skills or to learn how to build teams.

There is a more advanced type of coaching—the type I practice—in which the coach does not even talk about what the client would like to accomplish or what is holding them back.

---

*Gawande, Atul, 'Personal Best,' *The New Yorker*, 26 September 2011, https://tinyurl.com/495mwxyb. Accessed on 11 August 2023.

In fact, I do not even use the term 'coaching'. I prefer being a friend, philosopher and guide (FPG).

The function of an FPG is to engage with the client in a series of deep conversations on abstruse topics, such as the meaning of life and what it takes to be happy, where we come from and where we are going. The FPG does not prescribe a world view, but enables a client to refine his sense of self and become anchored in it. And, as the client gains clarity he goes on to do great things—things he would not even have conceived of but for the vistas opened to him by the FPG.

The best-known historical example of this is Aristotle and Alexander. When Aristotle, at the request of Philip of Macedonia, began to tutor Alexander, he did not instruct him on the finer points of swordsmanship or how to lay siege to an impregnable fortress. Instead, they talked about botany, geography and philosophy, and Aristotle introduced him to the glorious visions of Homeric poetry. They spent three years together, and at the end of that period Alexander began his remarkable saga of conquest and achievement.

When I work with leaders, I do not talk about specific skills they need to acquire. Instead, I lay out a philosophy of leadership and invite them to see how it fits into their world view and what the implications are for them, their organization and society.

Your business and career are merely a vehicle for your growth. It is not an end in itself. You use it as a tool to become the person you would like to be. This is why my approach is so extraordinarily effective for reflective individuals who realize that life is a spiritual journey.

Can you guess the secret to accomplishing phenomenal things while remaining as serene as a Zen monk? It is simple. But not easy. Strive with might and main to accomplish a great goal, but inwardly be completely at peace, no matter the outcome of your prodigious effort.

Invest in the process. Do not invest in the outcome. Paradoxically, the more you do so, the more likely you are to achieve your goals. Such an approach changes how you think, feel and behave in every area of your life.

Here is an example of how this works. One of my clients was fixated on offering great service to his customers. His team members were evaluated on client satisfaction scores. I asked him why he wanted to offer outstanding service, and he looked puzzled at being asked a question whose answer was so obvious.

He replied, 'Great service results in satisfied customers who will continue to buy from me. They may buy even more. They are more likely to refer me to their friends. As a result, my business will prosper.'

I invited him to consider if he had taken a noble impulse and converted it into a transaction. Did he really want to do that? How did that square with his spiritual growth?

'But why would I strive to offer great service if it did not bring me more business?' he asked, still puzzled.

'Because offering great service is the outward manifestation of the kind of person you are,' I suggested. 'Don't obsess about more business. That will happen organically. You do not have to give heed to it.'

'Why should my team give great service if they are not measured and compensated for it?' he asked.

'Because when they give great service, they know it. And they feel good about it. And they want to come to work and do it again and more of it,' I pointed out. 'It is your job to help them provide outstanding service and get rid of obstacles to their being able to do so.'

It took some time for him to anchor himself in this world view. His business from referrals doubled in the following year.

The reason my approach works is because I draw from the greatest masters the world has ever known. I have simply converted their teachings into practical, easily implementable steps. When you apply them, the one thing you can be sure about is that your results will improve exponentially.

The one thing you can be sure about is that your results will improve exponentially.

If you are already successful and are now ready to make a dent in the universe, you may wish to consider this remarkable new coaching. When you find the right FPG, the association will catapult you to higher orbits of achievement.

To explore further, go to https://theraoinstitute.com/coaching.